HOME OFFICE

Police and Criminal Evidence Act 1984 (s.66(1))

CODE OF PRACTICE C:
detention, treatment and questioning of persons by police officers

and

CODE OF PRACTICE H:
detention, treatment and questioning by police officers of persons under section 41 of, and Schedule 8 to, the Terrorism Act 2000

London: TSO

TSO

Published by TSO (The Stationery Office) and available from:

Online
www.tsoshop.co.uk
Mail, Telephone, Fax & E-mail

TSO
PO Box 29, Norwich, NR3 1GN
Telephone orders/General enquiries: 0870 600 5522
Fax orders: 0870 600 5533
E-mail: customer.services@tso.co.uk
Textphone 0870 240 3701

TSO Shops
123 Kingsway, London, WC2B 6PQ
020 7242 6393 Fax 020 7242 6394
68-69 Bull Street, Birmingham B4 6AD
0121 236 9696 Fax 0121 236 9699
9-21 Princess Street, Manchester M60 8AS
0161 834 7201 Fax 0161 833 0634
16 Arthur Street, Belfast BT1 4GD
028 9023 8451 Fax 028 9023 5401
18-19 High Street, Cardiff CF10 1PT
029 2039 5548 Fax 029 2038 4347
71 Lothian Road, Edinburgh EH3 9AZ
0870 606 5566 Fax 0870 606 5588

TSO Accredited Agents
(see Yellow Pages)
and through good booksellers

Published with the permission of the Home Office on behalf of Her Majesty's Stationery Office.

N5392390 c170 7/06

CONTENTS

H CODE OF PRACTICE IN CONNECTION WITH THE DETENTION, TREATMENT AND QUESTIONING BY POLICE OFFICERS OF PERSONS UNDER SECTION 41 OF, AND SCHEDULE 8 TO, THE TERRORISM ACT 2000

POLICE AND CRIMINAL EVIDENCE ACT 1984 (PACE)

CODE C

CODE OF PRACTICE FOR THE DETENTION, TREATMENT AND QUESTIONING OF PERSONS BY POLICE OFFICERS

Commencement – Transitional Arrangements

This Code applies to people in police detention after midnight on 24 July 2006, notwithstanding that their period of detention may have commenced before that time.

1   General

1.1   All persons in custody must be dealt with expeditiously, and released as soon as the need for detention no longer applies.

1.1A   A custody officer must perform the functions in this Code as soon as practicable. A custody officer will not be in breach of this Code if delay is justifiable and reasonable steps are taken to prevent unnecessary delay. The custody record shall show when a delay has occurred and the reason. See *Note 1H*

1.2   This Code of Practice must be readily available at all police stations for consultation by:

- police officers

- police staff

- detained persons

- members of the public.

1.3   The provisions of this Code:

- include the *Annexes*

- do not include the *Notes for Guidance*.

1.4   If an officer has any suspicion, or is told in good faith, that a person of any age may be mentally disordered or otherwise mentally vulnerable, in the absence of clear evidence to dispel that suspicion, the person shall be treated as such for the purposes of this Code. See *Note 1G*

1.5   If anyone appears to be under 17, they shall be treated as a juvenile for the purposes of this Code in the absence of clear evidence that they are older.

1.6   If a person appears to be blind, seriously visually impaired, deaf, unable to read or speak or has difficulty orally because of a speech impediment, they shall be treated as such for the purposes of this Code in the absence of clear evidence to the contrary.

1.7   'The appropriate adult' means, in the case of a:

(a)   juvenile:

　　(i)   the parent, guardian or, if the juvenile is in local authority or voluntary organisation care, or is otherwise being looked after under the Children Act 1989, a person representing that authority or organisation;

　　(ii)   a social worker of a local authority social services department;

      (iii)   failing these, some other responsible adult aged 18 or over who is not a police officer or employed by the police.

  (b)   person who is mentally disordered or mentally vulnerable: See Note 1D

      (iv)   a relative, guardian or other person responsible for their care or custody;

      (v)   someone experienced in dealing with mentally disordered or mentally vulnerable people but who is not a police officer or employed by the police;

      (vi)   failing these, some other responsible adult aged 18 or over who is not a police officer or employed by the police.

C

1.8   If this Code requires a person be given certain information, they do not have to be given it if at the time they are incapable of understanding what is said, are violent or may become violent or in urgent need of medical attention, but they must be given it as soon as practicable.

1.9   References to a custody officer include any:-

-    police officer; or

-    designated staff custody officer acting in the exercise or performance of the powers and duties conferred or imposed on them by their designation,

      performing the functions of a custody officer. See *Note 1J*.

1.9A When this Code requires the prior authority or agreement of an officer of at least inspector or superintendent rank, that authority may be given by a sergeant or chief inspector authorised to perform the functions of the higher rank under the Police and Criminal Evidence Act 1984 (PACE), section 107.

1.10 Subject to *paragraph 1.12*, this Code applies to people in custody at police stations in England and Wales, whether or not they have been arrested, and to those removed to a police station as a place of safety under the Mental Health Act 1983, sections 135 and 136. *Section 15* applies solely to people in police detention, e.g. those brought to a police station under arrest or arrested at a police station for an offence after going there voluntarily.

1.11 People detained under the Terrorism Act 2000, Schedule 8 and section 41 and other provisions of that Act are not subject to any part of this Code. Such persons are subject to the Code of Practice for detention, treatment and questioning of persons by police officers detained under that Act.

1.12 This Code's provisions do not apply to people in custody:

(i) arrested on warrants issued in Scotland by officers under the Criminal Justice and Public Order Act 1994, section 136(2), or arrested or detained without warrant by officers from a police force in Scotland under section 137(2). In these cases, police powers and duties and the person's rights and entitlements whilst at a police station in England or Wales are the same as those in Scotland;

(ii) arrested under the Immigration and Asylum Act 1999, section 142(3) in order to have their fingerprints taken;

(iii) whose detention is authorised by an immigration officer under the Immigration Act 1971;

(iv) who are convicted or remanded prisoners held in police cells on behalf of the Prison Service under the Imprisonment (Temporary Provisions) Act 1980;

(v) not used

(vi) detained for searches under stop and search powers except as required by Code A.

The provisions on conditions of detention and treatment in *sections 8* and *9* must be considered as the minimum standards of treatment for such detainees.

1.13 In this Code:

(a) 'designated person' means a person other than a police officer, designated under the Police Reform Act 2002, Part 4 who has specified powers and duties of police officers conferred or imposed on them;

(b) reference to a police officer includes a designated person acting in the exercise or performance of the powers and duties conferred or imposed on them by their designation.

1.14 Designated persons are entitled to use reasonable force as follows:-

(a) when exercising a power conferred on them which allows a police officer exercising that power to use reasonable force, a designated person has the same entitlement to use force; and

(b) at other times when carrying out duties conferred or imposed on them that also entitle them to use reasonable force, for example:

- when at a police station carrying out the duty to keep detainees for whom they are responsible under control and to assist any other police officer or designated person to keep any detainee under control and to prevent their escape.

- when securing, or assisting any other police officer or designated person in securing, the detention of a person at a police station.

- when escorting, or assisting any other police officer or designated person in escorting, a detainee within a police station.

- for the purpose of saving life or limb; or

- preventing serious damage to property.

1.15 Nothing in this Code prevents the custody officer, or other officer given custody of the detainee, from allowing police staff who are not designated persons to carry out individual procedures or tasks at the police station if the law allows. However, the officer remains responsible for making sure the procedures and tasks are carried out correctly in accordance with the Codes of Practice. Any such person must be:

(a) a person employed by a police authority maintaining a police force and under the control and direction of the Chief Officer of that force;

(b) employed by a person with whom a police authority has a contract for the provision of services relating to persons arrested or otherwise in custody.

1.16 Designated persons and other police staff must have regard to any relevant provisions of the Codes of Practice.

1.17 References to pocket books include any official report book issued to police officers or other police staff.

Notes for guidance

1A Although certain sections of this Code apply specifically to people in custody at police stations, those there voluntarily to assist with an investigation should be treated with no less consideration, e.g. offered refreshments at appropriate times, and enjoy an absolute right to obtain legal advice or communicate with anyone outside the police station.

1B A person, including a parent or guardian, should not be an appropriate adult if they:

- are

    - suspected of involvement in the offence

    - the victim

– *a witness*

– *involved in the investigation*

- received admissions prior to attending to act as the appropriate adult.

Note: If a juvenile's parent is estranged from the juvenile, they should not be asked to act as the appropriate adult if the juvenile expressly and specifically objects to their presence.

1C *If a juvenile admits an offence to, or in the presence of, a social worker or member of a youth offending team other than during the time that person is acting as the juvenile's appropriate adult, another appropriate adult should be appointed in the interest of fairness.*

1D *In the case of people who are mentally disordered or otherwise mentally vulnerable, it may be more satisfactory if the appropriate adult is someone experienced or trained in their care rather than a relative lacking such qualifications. But if the detainee prefers a relative to a better qualified stranger or objects to a particular person their wishes should, if practicable, be respected.*

1E *A detainee should always be given an opportunity, when an appropriate adult is called to the police station, to consult privately with a solicitor in the appropriate adult's absence if they want. An appropriate adult is not subject to legal privilege.*

1F *A solicitor or independent custody visitor (formerly a lay visitor) present at the police station in that capacity may not be the appropriate adult.*

1G *'Mentally vulnerable' applies to any detainee who, because of their mental state or capacity, may not understand the significance of what is said, of questions or of their replies. 'Mental disorder' is defined in the Mental Health Act 1983, section 1(2) as 'mental illness, arrested or incomplete development of mind, psychopathic disorder and any other disorder or disability of mind'. When the custody officer has any doubt about the mental state or capacity of a detainee, that detainee should be treated as mentally vulnerable and an appropriate adult called.*

1H *Paragraph 1.1A is intended to cover delays which may occur in processing detainees e.g. if:*

- a large number of suspects are brought into the station simultaneously to be placed in custody;

- interview rooms are all being used;

- there are difficulties contacting an appropriate adult, solicitor or interpreter.

1I   The custody officer must remind the appropriate adult and detainee about the right to legal advice and record any reasons for waiving it in accordance with section 6.

1J   The designation of police staff custody officers applies only in police areas where an order commencing the provisions of the Police Reform Act 2002, section 38 and Schedule 4A, for designating police staff custody officers is in effect.

1K   This Code does not affect the principle that all citizens have a duty to help police officers to prevent crime and discover offenders. This is a civic rather than a legal duty; but when a police officer is trying to discover whether, or by whom, an offence has been committed he is entitled to question any person from whom he thinks useful information can be obtained, subject to the restrictions imposed by this Code. A person's declaration that he is unwilling to reply does not alter this entitlement.

2   Custody records

2.1A   When a person is brought to a police station:

- under arrest

- is arrested at the police station having attended there voluntarily or

- attends a police station to answer bail

they should be brought before the custody officer as soon as practicable after their arrival at the station or, if appropriate, following arrest after attending the police station voluntarily. This applies to designated and non-designated police stations. A person is deemed to be "at a police station" for these purposes if they are within the boundary of any building or enclosed yard which forms part of that police station.

2.1   A separate custody record must be opened as soon as practicable for each person brought to a police station under arrest or arrested at the station having gone there voluntarily or attending a police station in answer to street bail. All information recorded under this Code must be recorded as soon as practicable in the custody record unless otherwise specified. Any audio or video recording made in the custody area is not part of the custody record.

2.2   If any action requires the authority of an officer of a specified rank, subject to *paragraph 2.6A*, their name and rank must be noted in the custody record.

2.3   The custody officer is responsible for the custody record's accuracy and completeness and for making sure the record or copy of the record accompanies a detainee if they are transferred to another police station. The record shall show the:

- time and reason for transfer;

C

- time a person is released from detention.

2.4 A solicitor or appropriate adult must be permitted to consult a detainee's custody record as soon as practicable after their arrival at the station and at any other time whilst the person is detained. Arrangements for this access must be agreed with the custody officer and may not unreasonably interfere with the custody officer's duties.

2.4A When a detainee leaves police detention or is taken before a court they, their legal representative or appropriate adult shall be given, on request, a copy of the custody record as soon as practicable. This entitlement lasts for 12 months after release.

2.5 The detainee, appropriate adult or legal representative shall be permitted to inspect the original custody record after the detainee has left police detention provided they give reasonable notice of their request. Any such inspection shall be noted in the custody record.

2.6 Subject to *paragraph 2.6A*, all entries in custody records must be timed and signed by the maker. Records entered on computer shall be timed and contain the operator's identification.

2.6A Nothing in this Code requires the identity of officers or other police staff to be recorded or disclosed:

(a) not used;

(b) if the officer or police staff reasonably believe recording or disclosing their name might put them in danger.

In these cases, they shall use their warrant or other identification numbers and the name of their police station. See *Note 2A*

2.7 The fact and time of any detainee's refusal to sign a custody record, when asked in accordance with this Code, must be recorded.

Note for guidance

2A *The purpose of paragraph 2.6A(b) is to protect those involved in serious organised crime investigations or arrests of particularly violent suspects when there is reliable information that those arrested or their associates may threaten or cause harm to those involved. In cases of doubt, an officer of inspector rank or above should be consulted.*

3   Initial action

(a)   Detained persons – normal procedure

3.1   When a person is brought to a police station under arrest or arrested at the station having gone there voluntarily, the custody officer must make sure the person is told clearly about the following continuing rights which may be exercised at any stage during the period in custody:

(i)   the right to have someone informed of their arrest as in *section 5*;

(ii)   the right to consult privately with a solicitor and that free independent legal advice is available;

(iii)   the right to consult these Codes of Practice. See *Note 3D*

3.2   The detainee must also be given:

* a written notice setting out:

    – the above three rights;

    – the arrangements for obtaining legal advice;

    – the right to a copy of the custody record as in *paragraph 2.4A*;

    – the caution in the terms prescribed in *section 10*.

* an additional written notice briefly setting out their entitlements while in custody, see *Notes 3A* and *3B*.

Note: The detainee shall be asked to sign the custody record to acknowledge receipt of these notices. Any refusal must be recorded on the custody record.

3.3   A citizen of an independent Commonwealth country or a national of a foreign country, including the Republic of Ireland, must be informed as soon as practicable about their rights of communication with their High Commission, Embassy or Consulate. See *section 7*

3.4   The custody officer shall:

* record the offence(s) that the detainee has been arrested for and the reason(s) for the arrest on the custody record. See *paragraph 10.3* and *Code G paragraphs 2.2* and *4.3*.

* note on the custody record any comment the detainee makes in relation to the arresting officer's account but shall not invite comment. If the arresting officer is not physically present when the detainee is brought to a police station, the

9

C

arresting officer's account must be made available to the custody officer remotely or by a third party on the arresting officer's behalf. If the custody officer authorises a person's detention the detainee must be informed of the grounds as soon as practicable and before they are questioned about any offence;

- note any comment the detainee makes in respect of the decision to detain them but shall not invite comment;

- not put specific questions to the detainee regarding their involvement in any offence, nor in respect of any comments they may make in response to the arresting officer's account or the decision to place them in detention. Such an exchange is likely to constitute an interview as in *paragraph 11.1A* and require the associated safeguards in *section 11*.

See *paragraph 11.13* in respect of unsolicited comments.

3.5 The custody officer shall:

(a) ask the detainee, whether at this time, they:

    (i) would like legal advice, see *paragraph 6.5*;

    (iii) want someone informed of their detention, see *section 5*;

(b) ask the detainee to sign the custody record to confirm their decisions in respect of (a);

(c) determine whether the detainee:

    (iii) is, or might be, in need of medical treatment or attention, see *section 9*;

    (iv) requires:

- an appropriate adult;

- help to check documentation;

- an interpreter;

(d) record the decision in respect of (c).

3.6 When determining these needs the custody officer is responsible for initiating an assessment to consider whether the detainee is likely to present specific risks to custody staff or themselves. Such assessments should always include a check on the Police National Computer, to be carried out as soon as practicable, to identify any risks highlighted in relation to the detainee. Although such assessments are primarily the custody officer's responsibility, it may be necessary for them to consult and involve others, e.g. the arresting officer or an appropriate health care professional, see *paragraph 9.13*. Reasons for delaying the initiation or completion of the assessment must be recorded.

3.7 Chief Officers should ensure that arrangements for proper and effective risk assessments required by *paragraph 3.6* are implemented in respect of all detainees at police stations in their area.

3.8 Risk assessments must follow a structured process which clearly defines the categories of risk to be considered and the results must be incorporated in the detainee's custody record. The custody officer is responsible for making sure those responsible for the detainee's custody are appropriately briefed about the risks. If no specific risks are identified by the assessment, that should be noted in the custody record. See *Note 3E* and *paragraph 9.14*

3.9 The custody officer is responsible for implementing the response to any specific risk assessment, e.g.:

- reducing opportunities for self harm;

- calling a health care professional;

- increasing levels of monitoring or observation.

3.10 Risk assessment is an ongoing process and assessments must always be subject to review if circumstances change.

3.11 If video cameras are installed in the custody area, notices shall be prominently displayed showing cameras are in use. Any request to have video cameras switched off shall be refused.

(b) Detained persons – special groups

3.12 If the detainee appears deaf or there is doubt about their hearing or speaking ability or ability to understand English, and the custody officer cannot establish effective communication, the custody officer must, as soon as practicable, call an interpreter for assistance in the action under *paragraphs 3.1–3.5*. See *section 13*

3.13 If the detainee is a juvenile, the custody officer must, if it is practicable, ascertain the identity of a person responsible for their welfare. That person:

- may be:

    - the parent or guardian;

C

- – if the juvenile is in local authority or voluntary organisation care, or is otherwise being looked after under the Children Act 1989, a person appointed by that authority or organisation to have responsibility for the juvenile's welfare;

- – any other person who has, for the time being, assumed responsibility for the juvenile's welfare.

- • must be informed as soon as practicable that the juvenile has been arrested, why they have been arrested and where they are detained. This right is in addition to the juvenile's right in *section 5* not to be held incommunicado. See *Note 3C*

3.14 If a juvenile is known to be subject to a court order under which a person or organisation is given any degree of statutory responsibility to supervise or otherwise monitor them, reasonable steps must also be taken to notify that person or organisation (the 'responsible officer'). The responsible officer will normally be a member of a Youth Offending Team, except for a curfew order which involves electronic monitoring when the contractor providing the monitoring will normally be the responsible officer.

3.15 If the detainee is a juvenile, mentally disordered or otherwise mentally vulnerable, the custody officer must, as soon as practicable:

- • inform the appropriate adult, who in the case of a juvenile may or may not be a person responsible for their welfare, as in *paragraph 3.13*, of:

  - – the grounds for their detention;

  - – their whereabouts.

- • ask the adult to come to the police station to see the detainee.

3.16 It is imperative that a mentally disordered or otherwise mentally vulnerable person, detained under the Mental Health Act 1983, section 136, be assessed as soon as possible. If that assessment is to take place at the police station, an approved social worker and a registered medical practitioner shall be called to the station as soon as possible in order to interview and examine the detainee. Once the detainee has been interviewed, examined and suitable arrangements made for their treatment or care, they can no longer be detained under section 136. A detainee must be immediately discharged from detention under section 136 if a registered medical practitioner, having examined them, concludes they are not mentally disordered within the meaning of the Act.

3.17 If the appropriate adult is:

- already at the police station, the provisions of *paragraphs 3.1* to *3.5* must be complied with in the appropriate adult's presence;

- not at the station when these provisions are complied with, they must be complied with again in the presence of the appropriate adult when they arrive.

3.18 The detainee shall be advised that:

- the duties of the appropriate adult include giving advice and assistance;

- they can consult privately with the appropriate adult at any time.

3.19 If the detainee, or appropriate adult on the detainee's behalf, asks for a solicitor to be called to give legal advice, the provisions of *section 6* apply.

3.20 If the detainee is blind, seriously visually impaired or unable to read, the custody officer shall make sure their solicitor, relative, appropriate adult or some other person likely to take an interest in them and not involved in the investigation is available to help check any documentation. When this Code requires written consent or signing the person assisting may be asked to sign instead, if the detainee prefers. This paragraph does not require an appropriate adult to be called solely to assist in checking and signing documentation for a person who is not a juvenile, or mentally disordered or otherwise mentally vulnerable (see *paragraph 3.15*).

(c)   Persons attending a police station voluntarily

3.21 Anybody attending a police station voluntarily to assist with an investigation may leave at will unless arrested. See *Note 1K*. If it is decided they shall not be allowed to leave, they must be informed at once that they are under arrest and brought before the custody officer, who is responsible for making sure they are notified of their rights in the same way as other detainees. If they are not arrested but are cautioned as in *section 10*, the person who gives the caution must, at the same time, inform them they are not under arrest, they are not obliged to remain at the station but if they remain at the station they may obtain free and independent legal advice if they want. They shall be told the right to legal advice includes the right to speak with a solicitor on the telephone and be asked if they want to do so.

3.22 If a person attending the police station voluntarily asks about their entitlement to legal advice, they shall be given a copy of the notice explaining the arrangements for obtaining legal advice. See *paragraph 3.2*

C

(d)   Documentation

3.23   The grounds for a person's detention shall be recorded, in the person's presence if practicable.

3.24   Action taken under *paragraphs 3.12* to *3.20* shall be recorded.

(e)   Persons answering street bail

3.25   When a person is answering street bail, the custody officer should link any documentation held in relation to arrest with the custody record. Any further action shall be recorded on the custody record in accordance with paragraphs 3.23 and 3.24 above.

Notes for guidance

3A   *The notice of entitlements should:*

- *list the entitlements in this Code, including:*

  - *visits and contact with outside parties, including special provisions for Commonwealth citizens and foreign nationals;*

  - *reasonable standards of physical comfort;*

  - *adequate food and drink;*

  - *access to toilets and washing facilities, clothing, medical attention, and exercise when practicable.*

- *mention the:*

  - *provisions relating to the conduct of interviews;*

  - *circumstances in which an appropriate adult should be available to assist the detainee and their statutory rights to make representation whenever the period of their detention is reviewed.*

3B   *In addition to notices in English, translations should be available in Welsh, the main minority ethnic languages and the principal European languages, whenever they are likely to be helpful. Audio versions of the notice should also be made available.*

3C   *If the juvenile is in local authority or voluntary organisation care but living with their parents or other adults responsible for their welfare, although there is no legal obligation to inform them, they should normally be contacted, as well as the authority or organisation unless suspected of involvement in the offence concerned. Even if the juvenile is not living with their parents, consideration should be given to informing them.*

3D   *The right to consult the Codes of Practice does not entitle the person concerned to delay unreasonably any necessary investigative or administrative action whilst they do so. Examples of action which need not be delayed unreasonably include:*

- *procedures requiring the provision of breath, blood or urine specimens under the Road Traffic Act 1988 or the Transport and Works Act 1992;*

- *searching detainees at the police station;*

- *taking fingerprints, footwear impressions or non-intimate samples without consent for evidential purposes.*

3E   *Home Office Circular 32/2000 provides more detailed guidance on risk assessments and identifies key risk areas which should always be considered.*

4   Detainee's property

(a)   Action

4.1   The custody officer is responsible for:

(a)   ascertaining what property a detainee:

   (i)   has with them when they come to the police station, whether on:

   - arrest or re-detention on answering to bail;

   - commitment to prison custody on the order or sentence of a court;

   - lodgement at the police station with a view to their production in court from prison custody;

   - transfer from detention at another station or hospital;

   - detention under the Mental Health Act 1983, section 135 or 136;

   - remand into police custody on the authority of a court

   (ii)   might have acquired for an unlawful or harmful purpose while in custody;

(b)   the safekeeping of any property taken from a detainee which remains at the police station.

The custody officer may search the detainee or authorise their being searched to the extent they consider necessary, provided a search of intimate parts of the body or involving the removal of more than outer clothing is only made as in *Annex A*. A search may only be carried out by an officer of the same sex as the detainee. See *Note 4A*

15

4.2   Detainees may retain clothing and personal effects at their own risk unless the custody officer considers they may use them to cause harm to themselves or others, interfere with evidence, damage property, effect an escape or they are needed as evidence. In this event the custody officer may withhold such articles as they consider necessary and must tell the detainee why.

4.3   Personal effects are those items a detainee may lawfully need, use or refer to while in detention but do not include cash and other items of value.

(b)   Documentation

4.4   It is a matter for the custody officer to determine whether a record should be made of the property a detained person has with him or had taken from him on arrest. Any record made is not required to be kept as part of the custody record but the custody record should be noted as to where such a record exists. Whenever a record is made the detainee shall be allowed to check and sign the record of property as correct. Any refusal to sign shall be recorded.

4.5   If a detainee is not allowed to keep any article of clothing or personal effects, the reason must be recorded.

Notes for guidance

4A   PACE, Section 54(1) and paragraph 4.1 require a detainee to be searched when it is clear the custody officer will have continuing duties in relation to that detainee or when that detainee's behaviour or offence makes an inventory appropriate. They do not require every detainee to be searched, e.g. if it is clear a person will only be detained for a short period and is not to be placed in a cell, the custody officer may decide not to search them. In such a case the custody record will be endorsed 'not searched', paragraph 4.4 will not apply, and the detainee will be invited to sign the entry. If the detainee refuses, the custody officer will be obliged to ascertain what property they have in accordance with paragraph 4.1.

4B   Paragraph 4.4 does not require the custody officer to record on the custody record property in the detainee's possession on arrest if, by virtue of its nature, quantity or size, it is not practicable to remove it to the police station.

4C   Paragraph 4.4 does not require items of clothing worn by the person be recorded unless withheld by the custody officer as in paragraph 4.2.

5   Right not to be held incommunicado

(a)   Action

5.1   Any person arrested and held in custody at a police station or other premises may, on request, have one person known to them or likely to take an interest in their welfare informed at public expense of their whereabouts as soon as practicable. If the person cannot be contacted the detainee may choose up to two alternatives. If they cannot be contacted, the person in charge of detention or the investigation has discretion to allow further attempts until the information has been conveyed. See *Notes 5C* and *5D*

5.2   The exercise of the above right in respect of each person nominated may be delayed only in accordance with *Annex B*.

5.3   The above right may be exercised each time a detainee is taken to another police station

5.4   The detainee may receive visits at the custody officer's discretion. See *Note 5B*

5.5   If a friend, relative or person with an interest in the detainee's welfare enquires about their whereabouts, this information shall be given if the suspect agrees and *Annex B* does not apply. See *Note 5D*

5.6   The detainee shall be given writing materials, on request, and allowed to telephone one person for a reasonable time, see *Notes 5A* and *5E*. Either or both these privileges may be denied or delayed if an officer of inspector rank or above considers sending a letter or making a telephone call may result in any of the consequences in:

(a)   *Annex B paragraphs 1* and *2* and the person is detained in connection with an indictable offence;

(b)   *Not used*

Nothing in this paragraph permits the restriction or denial of the rights in *paragraphs 5.1* and *6.1*.

5.7   Before any letter or message is sent, or telephone call made, the detainee shall be informed that what they say in any letter, call or message (other than in a communication to a solicitor) may be read or listened to and may be given in evidence. A telephone call may be terminated if it is being abused. The costs can be at public expense at the custody officer's discretion.

5.7A   Any delay or denial of the rights in this section should be proportionate and should last no longer than necessary.

C

(b)   Documentation

5.8   A record must be kept of any:

(a)   request made under this section and the action taken;

(b)   letters, messages or telephone calls made or received or visit received;

(c)   refusal by the detainee to have information about them given to an outside enquirer. The detainee must be asked to countersign the record accordingly and any refusal recorded.

Notes for guidance

5A   *A person may request an interpreter to interpret a telephone call or translate a letter.*

5B   *At the custody officer's discretion, visits should be allowed when possible, subject to having sufficient personnel to supervise a visit and any possible hindrance to the investigation.*

5C   *If the detainee does not know anyone to contact for advice or support or cannot contact a friend or relative, the custody officer should bear in mind any local voluntary bodies or other organisations who might be able to help. Paragraph 6.1 applies if legal advice is required.*

5D   *In some circumstances it may not be appropriate to use the telephone to disclose information under paragraphs 5.1 and 5.5.*

5E   *The telephone call at paragraph 5.6 is in addition to any communication under paragraphs 5.1 and 6.1.*

6   Right to legal advice

(a)   Action

6.1   Unless *Annex B* applies, all detainees must be informed that they may at any time consult and communicate privately with a solicitor, whether in person, in writing or by telephone, and that free independent legal advice is available from the duty solicitor. See *paragraph 3.1, Note 6B* and *Note 6J*

6.2   Not Used

6.3   A poster advertising the right to legal advice must be prominently displayed in the charging area of every police station. See *Note 6H*

6.4 No police officer should, at any time, do or say anything with the intention of dissuading a detainee from obtaining legal advice.

6.5 The exercise of the right of access to legal advice may be delayed only as in *Annex B*. Whenever legal advice is requested, and unless *Annex B* applies, the custody officer must act without delay to secure the provision of such advice. If, on being informed or reminded of this right, the detainee declines to speak to a solicitor in person, the officer should point out that the right includes the right to speak with a solicitor on the telephone. If the detainee continues to waive this right the officer should ask them why and any reasons should be recorded on the custody record or the interview record as appropriate. Reminders of the right to legal advice must be given as in *paragraphs 3.5, 11.2, 15.4, 16.4, 2B of Annex A, 3 of Annex K* and *16.5* and Code D, *paragraphs 3.17(ii)* and *6.3*. Once it is clear a detainee does not want to speak to a solicitor in person or by telephone they should cease to be asked their reasons. See *Note 6K*

6.5A In the case of a juvenile, an appropriate adult should consider whether legal advice from a solicitor is required. If the juvenile indicates that they do not want legal advice, the appropriate adult has the right to ask for a solicitor to attend if this would be in the best interests of the person. However, the detained person cannot be forced to see the solicitor if he is adamant that he does not wish to do so.

6.6 A detainee who wants legal advice may not be interviewed or continue to be interviewed until they have received such advice unless:

(a) *Annex B* applies, when the restriction on drawing adverse inferences from silence in *Annex C* will apply because the detainee is not allowed an opportunity to consult a solicitor; or

(b) an officer of superintendent rank or above has reasonable grounds for believing that:

    (i) the consequent delay might:

- lead to interference with, or harm to, evidence connected with an offence;

- lead to interference with, or physical harm to, other people;

- lead to serious loss of, or damage to, property;

- lead to alerting other people suspected of having committed an offence but not yet arrested for it;

- hinder the recovery of property obtained in consequence of the commission of an offence.

C

(ii)   when a solicitor, including a duty solicitor, has been contacted and has agreed to attend, awaiting their arrival would cause unreasonable delay to the process of investigation.

Note: In these cases the restriction on drawing adverse inferences from silence in *Annex C* will apply because the detainee is not allowed an opportunity to consult a solicitor.

(c)   the solicitor the detainee has nominated or selected from a list:

(i)   cannot be contacted;

(ii)   has previously indicated they do not wish to be contacted; or

(iii)   having been contacted, has declined to attend; and

the detainee has been advised of the Duty Solicitor Scheme but has declined to ask for the duty solicitor.

In these circumstances the interview may be started or continued without further delay provided an officer of inspector rank or above has agreed to the interview proceeding.

Note: The restriction on drawing adverse inferences from silence in Annex C will not apply because the detainee is allowed an opportunity to consult the duty solicitor;

(d)   the detainee changes their mind, about wanting legal advice.

In these circumstances the interview may be started or continued without delay provided that:

(i)   the detainee agrees to do so , in writing or on the interview record made in accordance with Code E or F; and

(ii)   an officer of inspector rank or above has inquired about the detainee's reasons for their change of mind and gives authority for the interview to proceed.

Confirmation of the detainee's agreement, their change of mind, the reasons for it if given and, subject to *paragraph 2.6A,* the name of the authorising officer shall be recorded in the written interview record or the interview record made in accordance with Code E or F. See *Note 6I.* Note: In these circumstances the restriction on drawing adverse inferences from silence in *Annex C* will not apply because the detainee is allowed an opportunity to consult a solicitor if they wish.

6.7   If *paragraph 6.6(b)(i)* applies, once sufficient information has been obtained to avert the risk, questioning must cease until the detainee has received legal advice unless *paragraph 6.6(a), (b)(ii), (c)* or *(d)* applies.

6.8   A detainee who has been permitted to consult a solicitor shall be entitled on request to have the solicitor present when they are interviewed unless one of the exceptions in *paragraph 6.6* applies.

6.9   The solicitor may only be required to leave the interview if their conduct is such that the interviewer is unable properly to put questions to the suspect. See *Notes 6D and 6E*

6.10   If the interviewer considers a solicitor is acting in such a way, they will stop the interview and consult an officer not below superintendent rank, if one is readily available, and otherwise an officer not below inspector rank not connected with the investigation. After speaking to the solicitor, the officer consulted will decide if the interview should continue in the presence of that solicitor. If they decide it should not, the suspect will be given the opportunity to consult another solicitor before the interview continues and that solicitor given an opportunity to be present at the interview. See *Note 6E*

6.11   The removal of a solicitor from an interview is a serious step and, if it occurs, the officer of superintendent rank or above who took the decision will consider if the incident should be reported to the Law Society. If the decision to remove the solicitor has been taken by an officer below superintendent rank, the facts must be reported to an officer of superintendent rank or above who will similarly consider whether a report to the Law Society would be appropriate. When the solicitor concerned is a duty solicitor, the report should be both to the Law Society and to the Legal Services Commission.

6.12   'Solicitor' in this Code means:

- a solicitor who holds a current practising certificate

- an accredited or probationary representative included on the register of representatives maintained by the Legal Services Commission.

6.12A An accredited or probationary representative sent to provide advice by, and on behalf of, a solicitor shall be admitted to the police station for this purpose unless an officer of inspector rank or above considers such a visit will hinder the investigation and directs otherwise. Hindering the investigation does not include giving proper legal advice to a detainee as in *Note 6D*. Once admitted to the police station, *paragraphs 6.6* to *6.10* apply.

21

6.13   In exercising their discretion under *paragraph 6.12A*, the officer should take into account in particular:

- whether:

    – the identity and status of an accredited or probationary representative have been satisfactorily established;

    – they are of suitable character to provide legal advice, e.g. a person with a criminal record is unlikely to be suitable unless the conviction was for a minor offence and not recent.

- any other matters in any written letter of authorisation provided by the solicitor on whose behalf the person is attending the police station. See *Note 6F*

6.14   If the inspector refuses access to an accredited or probationary representative or a decision is taken that such a person should not be permitted to remain at an interview, the inspector must notify the solicitor on whose behalf the representative was acting and give them an opportunity to make alternative arrangements. The detainee must be informed and the custody record noted.

6.15   If a solicitor arrives at the station to see a particular person, that person must, unless *Annex B* applies, be so informed whether or not they are being interviewed and asked if they would like to see the solicitor. This applies even if the detainee has declined legal advice or, having requested it, subsequently agreed to be interviewed without receiving advice. The solicitor's attendance and the detainee's decision must be noted in the custody record.

(b)   Documentation

6.16   Any request for legal advice and the action taken shall be recorded.

6.17   A record shall be made in the interview record if a detainee asks for legal advice and an interview is begun either in the absence of a solicitor or their representative, or they have been required to leave an interview.

Notes for guidance

6A   *In considering if paragraph 6.6(b) applies, the officer should, if practicable, ask the solicitor for an estimate of how long it will take to come to the station and relate this to the time detention is permitted, the time of day (i.e. whether the rest period under paragraph 12.2 is imminent) and the requirements of other investigations. If the solicitor is on their way or is to set off immediately, it will not normally be appropriate to begin an interview before they arrive. If it appears necessary to begin an interview before the* solicitor's arrival, they should be given an indication of how long the police would be able to wait before 6.6(b) applies so there is an opportunity to make arrangements for someone else to provide legal advice.

6B A detainee who asks for legal advice should be given an opportunity to consult a specific solicitor or another solicitor from that solicitor's firm or the duty solicitor. If advice is not available by these means, or they do not want to consult the duty solicitor, the detainee should be given an opportunity to choose a solicitor from a list of those willing to provide legal advice. If this solicitor is unavailable, they may choose up to two alternatives. If these attempts are unsuccessful, the custody officer has discretion to allow further attempts until a solicitor has been contacted and agrees to provide legal advice. Apart from carrying out these duties, an officer must not advise the suspect about any particular firm of solicitors.

6C Not Used

6D A detainee has a right to free legal advice and to be represented by a solicitor. The solicitor's only role in the police station is to protect and advance the legal rights of their client. On occasions this may require the solicitor to give advice which has the effect of the client avoiding giving evidence which strengthens a prosecution case. The solicitor may intervene in order to seek clarification, challenge an improper question to their client or the manner in which it is put, advise their client not to reply to particular questions, or if they wish to give their client further legal advice. Paragraph 6.9 only applies if the solicitor's approach or conduct prevents or unreasonably obstructs proper questions being put to the suspect or the suspect's response being recorded. Examples of unacceptable conduct include answering questions on a suspect's behalf or providing written replies for the suspect to quote.

6E An officer who takes the decision to exclude a solicitor must be in a position to satisfy the court the decision was properly made. In order to do this they may need to witness what is happening.

6F If an officer of at least inspector rank considers a particular solicitor or firm of solicitors is persistently sending probationary representatives who are unsuited to provide legal advice, they should inform an officer of at least superintendent rank, who may wish to take the matter up with the Law Society.

6G Subject to the constraints of Annex B, a solicitor may advise more than one client in an investigation if they wish. Any question of a conflict of interest is for the solicitor under their professional code of conduct. If, however, waiting for a solicitor to give advice to one client may lead to unreasonable delay to the interview with another, the provisions of paragraph 6.6(b) may apply.

C

6H   *In addition to a poster in English, a poster or posters containing translations into Welsh, the main minority ethnic languages and the principal European languages should be displayed wherever they are likely to be helpful and it is practicable to do so.*

6I   *Paragraph 6.6(d) requires the authorisation of an officer of inspector rank or above to the continuation of an interview when a detainee who wanted legal advice changes their mind. It is permissible for such authorisation to be given over the telephone, if the authorising officer is able to satisfy themselves about the reason for the detainee's change of mind and is satisfied it is proper to continue the interview in those circumstances.*

6J   *Whenever a detainee exercises their right to legal advice by consulting or communicating with a solicitor, they must be allowed to do so in private. This right to consult or communicate in private is fundamental. If the requirement for privacy is compromised because what is said or written by the detainee or solicitor for the purpose of giving and receiving legal advice is overheard, listened to, or read by others without the informed consent of the detainee, the right will effectively have been denied. When a detainee chooses to speak to a solicitor on the telephone, they should be allowed to do so in private unless this is impractical because of the design and layout of the custody area or the location of telephones. However, the normal expectation should be that facilities will be available, unless they are being used, at all police stations to enable detainees to speak in private to a solicitor either face to face or over the telephone.*

6K   *A detainee is not obliged to give reasons for declining legal advice and should not be pressed to do so.*

7   Citizens of independent Commonwealth countries or foreign nationals

(a)   Action

7.1   Any citizen of an independent Commonwealth country or a national of a foreign country, including the Republic of Ireland, may communicate at any time with the appropriate High Commission, Embassy or Consulate. The detainee must be informed as soon as practicable of:

- this right;

- their right, upon request, to have their High Commission, Embassy or Consulate told of their whereabouts and the grounds for their detention. Such a request should be acted upon as soon as practicable.

7.2   If a detainee is a citizen of a country with which a bilateral consular convention or agreement is in force requiring notification of arrest, the appropriate High Commission,

Embassy or Consulate shall be informed as soon as practicable, subject to *paragraph 7.4*. The countries to which this applies as at 1 April 2003 are listed in *Annex F*.

7.3   Consular officers may visit one of their nationals in police detention to talk to them and, if required, to arrange for legal advice. Such visits shall take place out of the hearing of a police officer.

7.4   Notwithstanding the provisions of consular conventions, if the detainee is a political refugee whether for reasons of race, nationality, political opinion or religion, or is seeking political asylum, consular officers shall not be informed of the arrest of one of their nationals or given access or information about them except at the detainee's express request.

C

(b)   Documentation

7.5   A record shall be made when a detainee is informed of their rights under this section and of any communications with a High Commission, Embassy or Consulate.

Note for guidance

7A   *The exercise of the rights in this section may not be interfered with even though Annex B applies.*

8   Conditions of detention

(a)   Action

8.1   So far as it is practicable, not more than one detainee should be detained in each cell.

8.2   Cells in use must be adequately heated, cleaned and ventilated. They must be adequately lit, subject to such dimming as is compatible with safety and security to allow people detained overnight to sleep. No additional restraints shall be used within a locked cell unless absolutely necessary and then only restraint equipment, approved for use in that force by the Chief Officer, which is reasonable and necessary in the circumstances having regard to the detainee's demeanour and with a view to ensuring their safety and the safety of others. If a detainee is deaf, mentally disordered or otherwise mentally vulnerable, particular care must be taken when deciding whether to use any form of approved restraints.

8.3   Blankets, mattresses, pillows and other bedding supplied shall be of a reasonable standard and in a clean and sanitary condition. See *Note 8A*

8.4   Access to toilet and washing facilities must be provided.

8.5   If it is necessary to remove a detainee's clothes for the purposes of investigation, for hygiene, health reasons or cleaning, replacement clothing of a reasonable standard of comfort and cleanliness shall be provided. A detainee may not be interviewed unless adequate clothing has been offered.

8.6   At least two light meals and one main meal should be offered in any 24 hour period. See *Note 8B*. Drinks should be provided at meal times and upon reasonable request between meals. Whenever necessary, advice shall be sought from the appropriate health care professional, see *Note 9A*, on medical and dietary matters. As far as practicable, meals provided shall offer a varied diet and meet any specific dietary needs or religious beliefs the detainee may have. The detainee may, at the custody officer's discretion, have meals supplied by their family or friends at their expense. See *Note 8A*

8.7   Brief outdoor exercise shall be offered daily if practicable.

8.8   A juvenile shall not be placed in a police cell unless no other secure accommodation is available and the custody officer considers it is not practicable to supervise them if they are not placed in a cell or that a cell provides more comfortable accommodation than other secure accommodation in the station. A juvenile may not be placed in a cell with a detained adult.

(b)   Documentation

8.9   A record must be kept of replacement clothing and meals offered.

8.10   If a juvenile is placed in a cell, the reason must be recorded.

8.11   The use of any restraints on a detainee whilst in a cell, the reasons for it and, if appropriate, the arrangements for enhanced supervision of the detainee whilst so restrained, shall be recorded. See *paragraph 3.9*

Notes for guidance

8A   *The provisions in paragraph 8.3 and 8.6 respectively are of particular importance in the case of a person likely to be detained for an extended period. In deciding whether to allow meals to be supplied by family or friends, the custody officer is entitled to take account of the risk of items being concealed in any food or package and the officer's duties and responsibilities under food handling legislation.*

8B   *Meals should, so far as practicable, be offered at recognised meal times, or at other times that take account of when the detainee last had a meal.*

9 Care and treatment of detained persons

(a) General

9.1 Nothing in this section prevents the police from calling the police surgeon or, if appropriate, some other health care professional, to examine a detainee for the purposes of obtaining evidence relating to any offence in which the detainee is suspected of being involved. See *Note 9A*

9.2 If a complaint is made by, or on behalf of, a detainee about their treatment since their arrest, or it comes to notice that a detainee may have been treated improperly, a report must be made as soon as practicable to an officer of inspector rank or above not connected with the investigation. If the matter concerns a possible assault or the possibility of the unnecessary or unreasonable use of force, an appropriate health care professional must also be called as soon as practicable.

9.3 Detainees should be visited at least every hour. If no reasonably foreseeable risk was identified in a risk assessment, see *paragraphs 3.6 – 3.10*, there is no need to wake a sleeping detainee. Those suspected of being intoxicated through drink or drugs or having swallowed drugs, see *Note 9CA*, or whose level of consciousness causes concern must, subject to any clinical directions given by the appropriate health care professional, see *paragraph 9.13*:

- be visited and roused at least every half hour

- have their condition assessed as in *Annex H*

- and clinical treatment arranged if appropriate

See *Notes 9B, 9C* and *9H*

9.4 When arrangements are made to secure clinical attention for a detainee, the custody officer must make sure all relevant information which might assist in the treatment of the detainee's condition is made available to the responsible health care professional. This applies whether or not the health care professional asks for such information. Any officer or police staff with relevant information must inform the custody officer as soon as practicable.

(b) Clinical treatment and attention

9.5 The custody officer must make sure a detainee receives appropriate clinical attention as soon as reasonably practicable if the person:

(a) appears to be suffering from physical illness; or

(b)   is injured; or

(c)   appears to be suffering from a mental disorder; or

(d)   appears to need clinical attention

9.5A   This applies even if the detainee makes no request for clinical attention and whether or not they have already received clinical attention elsewhere. If the need for attention appears urgent, e.g. when indicated as in *Annex H*, the nearest available health care professional or an ambulance must be called immediately.

9.5B   The custody officer must also consider the need for clinical attention as set out in Note for Guidance 9C in relation to those suffering the effects of alcohol or drugs.

9.6   *Paragraph 9.5* is not meant to prevent or delay the transfer to a hospital if necessary of a person detained under the Mental Health Act 1983, section 136. See *Note 9D*. When an assessment under that Act takes place at a police station, see *paragraph 3.16*, the custody officer must consider whether an appropriate health care professional should be called to conduct an initial clinical check on the detainee. This applies particularly when there is likely to be any significant delay in the arrival of a suitably qualified medical practitioner.

9.7   If it appears to the custody officer, or they are told, that a person brought to a station under arrest may be suffering from an infectious disease or condition, the custody officer must take reasonable steps to safeguard the health of the detainee and others at the station. In deciding what action to take, advice must be sought from an appropriate health care professional. See *Note 9E*. The custody officer has discretion to isolate the person and their property until clinical directions have been obtained.

9.8   If a detainee requests a clinical examination, an appropriate health care professional must be called as soon as practicable to assess the detainee's clinical needs. If a safe and appropriate care plan cannot be provided, the police surgeon's advice must be sought. The detainee may also be examined by a medical practitioner of their choice at their expense.

9.9   If a detainee is required to take or apply any medication in compliance with clinical directions prescribed before their detention, the custody officer must consult the appropriate health care professional before the use of the medication. Subject to the restrictions in *paragraph 9.10,* the custody officer is responsible for the safekeeping of any medication and for making sure the detainee is given the opportunity to take or apply prescribed or approved medication. Any such consultation and its outcome shall be noted in the custody record.

9.10 No police officer may administer or supervise the self-administration of medically prescribed controlled drugs of the types and forms listed in the Misuse of Drugs Regulations 2001, Schedule 2 or 3. A detainee may only self-administer such drugs under the personal supervision of the registered medical practitioner authorising their use. Drugs listed in Schedule 4 or 5 may be distributed by the custody officer for self-administration if they have consulted the registered medical practitioner authorising their use, this may be done by telephone, and both parties are satisfied self-administration will not expose the detainee, police officers or anyone else to the risk of harm or injury.

9.11 When appropriate health care professionals administer drugs or other medications, or supervise their self-administration, it must be within current medicines legislation and the scope of practice as determined by their relevant professional body.

9.12 If a detainee has in their possession, or claims to need, medication relating to a heart condition, diabetes, epilepsy or a condition of comparable potential seriousness then, even though *paragraph 9.5* may not apply, the advice of the appropriate health care professional must be obtained.

9.13 Whenever the appropriate health care professional is called in accordance with this section to examine or treat a detainee, the custody officer shall ask for their opinion about:

- any risks or problems which police need to take into account when making decisions about the detainee's continued detention;

- when to carry out an interview if applicable; and

- the need for safeguards.

9.14 When clinical directions are given by the appropriate health care professional, whether orally or in writing, and the custody officer has any doubts or is in any way uncertain about any aspect of the directions, the custody officer shall ask for clarification. It is particularly important that directions concerning the frequency of visits are clear, precise and capable of being implemented. See *Note 9F*.

(c) Documentation

9.15 A record must be made in the custody record of:

(a) the arrangements made for an examination by an appropriate health care professional under *paragraph 9.2* and of any complaint reported under that paragraph together with any relevant remarks by the custody officer;

(b) any arrangements made in accordance with *paragraph 9.5*;

(c)   any request for a clinical examination under *paragraph 9.8* and any arrangements made in response;

(d)   the injury, ailment, condition or other reason which made it necessary to make the arrangements in (a) to (c), *see Note 9G*;

(e)   any clinical directions and advice, including any further clarifications, given to police by a health care professional concerning the care and treatment of the detainee in connection with any of the arrangements made in (a) to (c), *see Note 9F*;

(f)   if applicable, the responses received when attempting to rouse a person using the procedure in *Annex H, see Note 9H*.

9.16   If a health care professional does not record their clinical findings in the custody record, the record must show where they are recorded. See *Note 9G*. However, information which is necessary to custody staff to ensure the effective ongoing care and well being of the detainee must be recorded openly in the custody record, see *paragraph 3.8* and *Annex G, paragraph 7*.

9.17   Subject to the requirements of *Section 4*, the custody record shall include:

• a record of all medication a detainee has in their possession on arrival at the police station;

• a note of any such medication they claim to need but do not have with them.

Notes for guidance

9A   *A 'health care professional' means a clinically qualified person working within the scope of practice as determined by their relevant professional body. Whether a health care professional is 'appropriate' depends on the circumstances of the duties they carry out at the time.*

9B   *Whenever possible juveniles and mentally vulnerable detainees should be visited more frequently.*

9C   *A detainee who appears drunk or behaves abnormally may be suffering from illness, the effects of drugs or may have sustained injury, particularly a head injury which is not apparent. A detainee needing or dependent on certain drugs, including alcohol, may experience harmful effects within a short time of being deprived of their supply. In these circumstances, when there is any doubt, police should always act urgently to call an appropriate health care professional or an ambulance. Paragraph 9.5 does not apply to minor ailments or injuries which do not need attention. However, all such ailments*

30

or injuries must be recorded in the custody record and any doubt must be resolved in favour of calling the appropriate health care professional.

9CA Paragraph 9.3 would apply to a person in police custody by order of a magistrates' court under the Criminal Justice Act 1988, section 152 (as amended by the Drugs Act 2005, section 8) to facilitate the recovery of evidence after being charged with drug possession or drug trafficking and suspected of having swallowed drugs. In the case of the healthcare needs of a person who has swallowed drugs, the custody officer subject to any clinical directions, should consider the necessity for rousing every half hour. This does not negate the need for regular visiting of the suspect in the cell.

9D Whenever practicable, arrangements should be made for persons detained for assessment under the Mental Health Act 1983, section 136 to be taken to a hospital. There is no power under that Act to transfer a person detained under section 136 from one place of safety to another place of safety for assessment.

9E It is important to respect a person's right to privacy and information about their health must be kept confidential and only disclosed with their consent or in accordance with clinical advice when it is necessary to protect the detainee's health or that of others who come into contact with them.

9F The custody officer should always seek to clarify directions that the detainee requires constant observation or supervision and should ask the appropriate health care professional to explain precisely what action needs to be taken to implement such directions.

9G Paragraphs 9.15 and 9.16 do not require any information about the cause of any injury, ailment or condition to be recorded on the custody record if it appears capable of providing evidence of an offence.

9H The purpose of recording a person's responses when attempting to rouse them using the procedure in Annex H is to enable any change in the individual's consciousness level to be noted and clinical treatment arranged if appropriate.

10 Cautions

(a) When a caution must be given

10.1 A person whom there are grounds to suspect of an offence, see *Note 10A*, must be cautioned before any questions about an offence, or further questions if the answers provide the grounds for suspicion, are put to them if either the suspect's answers or silence, (i.e. failure or refusal to answer or answer satisfactorily) may be given in evidence to a court in a prosecution. A person need not be cautioned if questions are for other necessary purposes, e.g.:

(a)   solely to establish their identity or ownership of any vehicle;

(b)   to obtain information in accordance with any relevant statutory requirement, see *paragraph 10.9*;

(c)   in furtherance of the proper and effective conduct of a search, e.g. to determine the need to search in the exercise of powers of stop and search or to seek co-operation while carrying out a search;

(d)   to seek verification of a written record as in *paragraph 11.13*;

(e)   Not used

10.2   Whenever a person not under arrest is initially cautioned, or reminded they are under caution, that person must at the same time be told they are not under arrest and are free to leave if they want to. See *Note 10C*

10.3   A person who is arrested, or further arrested, must be informed at the time, or as soon as practicable thereafter, that they are under arrest and the grounds for their arrest, see paragraph 3.4, *Note 10B* and *Code G, paragraphs 2.2 and 4.3.*.

10.4   As per *Code G, section 3*, a person who is arrested, or further arrested, must also be cautioned unless:

(a)   it is impracticable to do so by reason of their condition or behaviour at the time;

(b)   they have already been cautioned immediately prior to arrest as in *paragraph 10.1.*

(b)   Terms of the cautions

10.5   The caution which must be given on:

(a)   arrest;

(b)   all other occasions before a person is charged or informed they may be prosecuted, see *section 16*,

should, unless the restriction on drawing adverse inferences from silence applies, see *Annex C*, be in the following terms:

"You do not have to say anything. But it may harm your defence if you do not mention when questioned something which you later rely on in Court. Anything you do say may be given in evidence."

See *Note 10G*

10.6 *Annex C, paragraph 2* sets out the alternative terms of the caution to be used when the restriction on drawing adverse inferences from silence applies.

10.7 Minor deviations from the words of any caution given in accordance with this Code do not constitute a breach of this Code, provided the sense of the relevant caution is preserved. See *Note 10D*

10.8 After any break in questioning under caution, the person being questioned must be made aware they remain under caution. If there is any doubt the relevant caution should be given again in full when the interview resumes. See *Note 10E*

10.9 When, despite being cautioned, a person fails to co-operate or to answer particular questions which may affect their immediate treatment, the person should be informed of any relevant consequences and that those consequences are not affected by the caution. Examples are when a person's refusal to provide:

- their name and address when charged may make them liable to detention;

- particulars and information in accordance with a statutory requirement, e.g. under the Road Traffic Act 1988, may amount to an offence or may make the person liable to a further arrest.

(c) Special warnings under the Criminal Justice and Public Order Act 1994, sections 36 and 37

10.10 When a suspect interviewed at a police station or authorised place of detention after arrest fails or refuses to answer certain questions, or to answer satisfactorily, after due warning, see *Note 10F*, a court or jury may draw such inferences as appear proper under the Criminal Justice and Public Order Act 1994, sections 36 and 37. Such inferences may only be drawn when:

(a) the restriction on drawing adverse inferences from silence, see *Annex C*, does not apply; and

(b) the suspect is arrested by a constable and fails or refuses to account for any objects, marks or substances, or marks on such objects found:

- on their person;

- in or on their clothing or footwear;

- otherwise in their possession; or

- in the place they were arrested;

33

(c)   the arrested suspect was found by a constable at a place at or about the time the offence for which that officer has arrested them is alleged to have been committed, and the suspect fails or refuses to account for their presence there.

When the restriction on drawing adverse inferences from silence applies, the suspect may still be asked to account for any of the matters in (*b*) or (*c*) but the special warning described in *paragraph 10.11* will not apply and must not be given.

10.11 For an inference to be drawn when a suspect fails or refuses to answer a question about one of these matters or to answer it satisfactorily, the suspect must first be told in ordinary language:

(a)   what offence is being investigated;

(b)   what fact they are being asked to account for;

(c)   this fact may be due to them taking part in the commission of the offence;

(d)   a court may draw a proper inference if they fail or refuse to account for this fact;

(e)   a record is being made of the interview and it may be given in evidence if they are brought to trial.

(d)   *Juveniles and persons who are mentally disordered or otherwise mentally vulnerable*

10.12 If a juvenile or a person who is mentally disordered or otherwise mentally vulnerable is cautioned in the absence of the appropriate adult, the caution must be repeated in the adult's presence.

(e)   *Documentation*

10.13 A record shall be made when a caution is given under this section, either in the interviewer's pocket book or in the interview record.

Notes for guidance

10A   There must be some reasonable, objective grounds for the suspicion, based on known facts or information which are relevant to the likelihood the offence has been committed and the person to be questioned committed it.

10B   An arrested person must be given sufficient information to enable them to understand that they have been deprived of their liberty and the reason they have been arrested, e.g. when a person is arrested on suspicion of committing an offence they must be informed of the suspected offence's nature, when and where it was committed. The suspect must also be informed of the reason or reasons why the arrest is considered necessary. Vague or technical language should be avoided.

10C   The restriction on drawing inferences from silence, see Annex C, paragraph 1, does not apply to a person who has not been detained and who therefore cannot be prevented from seeking legal advice if they want, see paragraph 3.21.

10D   If it appears a person does not understand the caution, the person giving it should explain it in their own words.

10E   It may be necessary to show to the court that nothing occurred during an interview break or between interviews which influenced the suspect's recorded evidence. After a break in an interview or at the beginning of a subsequent interview, the interviewing officer should summarise the reason for the break and confirm this with the suspect.

10F   The Criminal Justice and Public Order Act 1994, sections 36 and 37 apply only to suspects who have been arrested by a constable or Customs and Excise officer and are given the relevant warning by the police or customs officer who made the arrest or who is investigating the offence. They do not apply to any interviews with suspects who have not been arrested.

10G   Nothing in this Code requires a caution to be given or repeated when informing a person not under arrest they may be prosecuted for an offence. However, a court will not be able to draw any inferences under the Criminal Justice and Public Order Act 1994, section 34, if the person was not cautioned.

11   Interviews – general

(a)   Action

11.1A An interview is the questioning of a person regarding their involvement or suspected involvement in a criminal offence or offences which, under paragraph 10.1, must be carried out under caution. Whenever a person is interviewed they must be informed of the nature of the offence, or further offence. Procedures under the Road Traffic Act 1988, section 7 or the Transport and Works Act 1992, section 31 do not constitute interviewing for the purpose of this Code.

11.1   Following a decision to arrest a suspect, they must not be interviewed about the relevant offence except at a police station or other authorised place of detention, unless the consequent delay would be likely to:

(a)   lead to:

•   interference with, or harm to, evidence connected with an offence;

- interference with, or physical harm to, other people; or

- serious loss of, or damage to, property;

(b)　lead to alerting other people suspected of committing an offence but not yet arrested for it; or

(c)　hinder the recovery of property obtained in consequence of the commission of an offence.

Interviewing in any of these circumstances shall cease once the relevant risk has been averted or the necessary questions have been put in order to attempt to avert that risk.

11.2　Immediately prior to the commencement or re-commencement of any interview at a police station or other authorised place of detention, the interviewer should remind the suspect of their entitlement to free legal advice and that the interview can be delayed for legal advice to be obtained, unless one of the exceptions in *paragraph 6.6* applies. It is the interviewer's responsibility to make sure all reminders are recorded in the interview record.

11.3　Not Used

11.4　At the beginning of an interview the interviewer, after cautioning the suspect, see *section 10*, shall put to them any significant statement or silence which occurred in the presence and hearing of a police officer or other police staff before the start of the interview and which have not been put to the suspect in the course of a previous interview. See *Note 11A*. The interviewer shall ask the suspect whether they confirm or deny that earlier statement or silence and if they want to add anything.

11.4A A significant statement is one which appears capable of being used in evidence against the suspect, in particular a direct admission of guilt. A significant silence is a failure or refusal to answer a question or answer satisfactorily when under caution, which might, allowing for the restriction on drawing adverse inferences from silence, see *Annex C*, give rise to an inference under the Criminal Justice and Public Order Act 1994, Part III.

11.5　No interviewer may try to obtain answers or elicit a statement by the use of oppression. Except as in *paragraph 10.9*, no interviewer shall indicate, except to answer a direct question, what action will be taken by the police if the person being questioned answers questions, makes a statement or refuses to do either. If the person asks directly what action will be taken if they answer questions, make a statement or refuse to do either, the interviewer may inform them what action the police propose to take provided that action is itself proper and warranted.

11.6   The interview or further interview of a person about an offence with which that person has not been charged or for which they have not been informed they may be prosecuted, must cease when:

(a)   the officer in charge of the investigation is satisfied all the questions they consider relevant to obtaining accurate and reliable information about the offence have been put to the suspect, this includes allowing the suspect an opportunity to give an innocent explanation and asking questions to test if the explanation is accurate and reliable, e.g. to clear up ambiguities or clarify what the suspect said;

(b)   the officer in charge of the investigation has taken account of any other available evidence; and

(c)   the officer in charge of the investigation, or in the case of a detained suspect, the custody officer, see *paragraph 16.1*, reasonably believes there is sufficient evidence to provide a realistic prospect of conviction for that offence. *See Note 11B*

This paragraph does not prevent officers in revenue cases or acting under the confiscation provisions of the Criminal Justice Act 1988 or the Drug Trafficking Act 1994 from inviting suspects to complete a formal question and answer record after the interview is concluded.

(b)   Interview records

11.7   (a)   An accurate record must be made of each interview, whether or not the interview takes place at a police station

(b)   The record must state the place of interview, the time it begins and ends, any interview breaks and, subject to *paragraph 2.6A*, the names of all those present; and must be made on the forms provided for this purpose or in the interviewer's pocket book or in accordance with the Codes of Practice E or F;

(c)   Any written record must be made and completed during the interview, unless this would not be practicable or would interfere with the conduct of the interview, and must constitute either a verbatim record of what has been said or, failing this, an account of the interview which adequately and accurately summarises it.

11.8   If a written record is not made during the interview it must be made as soon as practicable after its completion.

11.9   Written interview records must be timed and signed by the maker.

C

11.10 If a written record is not completed during the interview the reason must be recorded in the interview record.

11.11 Unless it is impracticable, the person interviewed shall be given the opportunity to read the interview record and to sign it as correct or to indicate how they consider it inaccurate. If the person interviewed cannot read or refuses to read the record or sign it, the senior interviewer present shall read it to them and ask whether they would like to sign it as correct or make their mark or to indicate how they consider it inaccurate. The interviewer shall certify on the interview record itself what has occurred. See *Note 11E*

11.12 If the appropriate adult or the person's solicitor is present during the interview, they should also be given an opportunity to read and sign the interview record or any written statement taken down during the interview.

11.13 A written record shall be made of any comments made by a suspect, including unsolicited comments, which are outside the context of an interview but which might be relevant to the offence. Any such record must be timed and signed by the maker. When practicable the suspect shall be given the opportunity to read that record and to sign it as correct or to indicate how they consider it inaccurate. See *Note 11E*

11.14 Any refusal by a person to sign an interview record when asked in accordance with this Code must itself be recorded.

(c) *Juveniles and mentally disordered or otherwise mentally vulnerable people*

11.15 A juvenile or person who is mentally disordered or otherwise mentally vulnerable must not be interviewed regarding their involvement or suspected involvement in a criminal offence or offences, or asked to provide or sign a written statement under caution or record of interview, in the absence of the appropriate adult unless *paragraphs 11.1, 11.18* to *11.20* apply. See *Note 11C*

11.16 Juveniles may only be interviewed at their place of education in exceptional circumstances and only when the principal or their nominee agrees. Every effort should be made to notify the parent(s) or other person responsible for the juvenile's welfare and the appropriate adult, if this is a different person, that the police want to interview the juvenile and reasonable time should be allowed to enable the appropriate adult to be present at the interview. If awaiting the appropriate adult would cause unreasonable delay, and unless the juvenile is suspected of an offence against the educational establishment, the principal or their nominee can act as the appropriate adult for the purposes of the interview.

11.17 If an appropriate adult is present at an interview, they shall be informed:

- they are not expected to act simply as an observer; and

- the purpose of their presence is to:

    – advise the person being interviewed;

    – observe whether the interview is being conducted properly and fairly;

    – facilitate communication with the person being interviewed.

C

(d)   Vulnerable suspects – urgent interviews at police stations

11.18 The following persons may not be interviewed unless an officer of superintendent rank or above considers delay will lead to the consequences in *paragraph 11.1(a)* to *(c)*, and is satisfied the interview would not significantly harm the person's physical or mental state (see Annex G):

(a)   a juvenile or person who is mentally disordered or otherwise mentally vulnerable if at the time of the interview the appropriate adult is not present;

(b)   anyone other than in (a) who at the time of the interview appears unable to:

- appreciate the significance of questions and their answers; or

- understand what is happening because of the effects of drink, drugs or any illness, ailment or condition;

(c)   a person who has difficulty understanding English or has a hearing disability, if at the time of the interview an interpreter is not present.

11.19 These interviews may not continue once sufficient information has been obtained to avert the consequences in *paragraph 11.1(a)* to *(c)*.

11.20 A record shall be made of the grounds for any decision to interview a person under *paragraph 11.18*.

Notes for guidance

11A   *Paragraph 11.4 does not prevent the interviewer from putting significant statements and silences to a suspect again at a later stage or a further interview.*

11B   *The Criminal Procedure and Investigations Act 1996 Code of Practice, paragraph 3.4 states 'In conducting an investigation, the investigator should pursue all reasonable lines of enquiry, whether these point towards or away from the suspect. What is reasonable will depend on the particular circumstances.' Interviewers should keep this in mind when deciding what questions to ask in an interview.*

11C *Although juveniles or people who are mentally disordered or otherwise mentally vulnerable are often capable of providing reliable evidence, they may, without knowing or wishing to do so, be particularly prone in certain circumstances to provide information that may be unreliable, misleading or self-incriminating. Special care should always be taken when questioning such a person, and the appropriate adult should be involved if there is any doubt about a person's age, mental state or capacity. Because of the risk of unreliable evidence it is also important to obtain corroboration of any facts admitted whenever possible.*

11D *Juveniles should not be arrested at their place of education unless this is unavoidable. When a juvenile is arrested at their place of education, the principal or their nominee must be informed.*

11E *Significant statements described in paragraph 11.4 will always be relevant to the offence and must be recorded. When a suspect agrees to read records of interviews and other comments and sign them as correct, they should be asked to endorse the record with, e.g. 'I agree that this is a correct record of what was said' and add their signature. If the suspect does not agree with the record, the interviewer should record the details of any disagreement and ask the suspect to read these details and sign them to the effect that they accurately reflect their disagreement. Any refusal to sign should be recorded.*

12 Interviews in police stations

(a) Action

12.1 If a police officer wants to interview or conduct enquiries which require the presence of a detainee, the custody officer is responsible for deciding whether to deliver the detainee into the officer's custody.

12.2 Except as below, in any period of 24 hours a detainee must be allowed a continuous period of at least 8 hours for rest, free from questioning, travel or any interruption in connection with the investigation concerned. This period should normally be at night or other appropriate time which takes account of when the detainee last slept or rested. If a detainee is arrested at a police station after going there voluntarily, the period of 24 hours runs from the time of their arrest and not the time of arrival at the police station. The period may not be interrupted or delayed, except:

    (a)   when there are reasonable grounds for believing not delaying or interrupting the period would:

      (i)   involve a risk of harm to people or serious loss of, or damage to, property;

      (iii)   delay unnecessarily the person's release from custody;

      (iii)   otherwise prejudice the outcome of the investigation;

(b)   at the request of the detainee, their appropriate adult or legal representative;

(c)   when a delay or interruption is necessary in order to:

      (i)   comply with the legal obligations and duties arising under *section 15*;

      (ii)   to take action required under *section 9* or in accordance with medical advice.

If the period is interrupted in accordance with *(a)*, a fresh period must be allowed. Interruptions under *(b)* and *(c)*, do not require a fresh period to be allowed.

12.3   Before a detainee is interviewed the custody officer, in consultation with the officer in charge of the investigation and appropriate health care professionals as necessary, shall assess whether the detainee is fit enough to be interviewed. This means determining and considering the risks to the detainee's physical and mental state if the interview took place and determining what safeguards are needed to allow the interview to take place. See *Annex G*. The custody officer shall not allow a detainee to be interviewed if the custody officer considers it would cause significant harm to the detainee's physical or mental state. Vulnerable suspects listed at *paragraph 11.18* shall be treated as always being at some risk during an interview and these persons may not be interviewed except in accordance with *paragraphs 11.18* to *11.20*.

12.4   As far as practicable interviews shall take place in interview rooms which are adequately heated, lit and ventilated.

12.5   A suspect whose detention without charge has been authorised under PACE, because the detention is necessary for an interview to obtain evidence of the offence for which they have been arrested, may choose not to answer questions but police do not require the suspect's consent or agreement to interview them for this purpose. If a suspect takes steps to prevent themselves being questioned or further questioned, e.g. by refusing to leave their cell to go to a suitable interview room or by trying to leave the interview room, they shall be advised their consent or agreement to interview is not required. The suspect shall be cautioned as in *section 10*, and informed if they fail or refuse to co-operate, the interview may take place in the cell and that their failure or refusal to co-operate may be given in evidence. The suspect shall then be invited to co-operate and go into the interview room.

C

12.6 People being questioned or making statements shall not be required to stand.

12.7 Before the interview commences each interviewer shall, subject to *paragraph 2.6A*, identify themselves and any other persons present to the interviewee.

12.8 Breaks from interviewing should be made at recognised meal times or at other times that take account of when an interviewee last had a meal. Short refreshment breaks shall be provided at approximately two hour intervals, subject to the interviewer's discretion to delay a break if there are reasonable grounds for believing it would:

(i) involve a:

- risk of harm to people;

- serious loss of, or damage to, property;

(ii) unnecessarily delay the detainee's release;

(iii) otherwise prejudice the outcome of the investigation.

See *Note 12B*

12.9 If during the interview a complaint is made by or on behalf of the interviewee concerning the provisions of this Code, the interviewer should:

(i) record it in the interview record;

(ii) inform the custody officer, who is then responsible for dealing with it as in *section 9*.

(b) Documentation

12.10 A record must be made of the:

- time a detainee is not in the custody of the custody officer, and why

- reason for any refusal to deliver the detainee out of that custody

12.11 A record shall be made of:

(a) the reasons it was not practicable to use an interview room; and

(b) any action taken as in *paragraph 12.5*.

The record shall be made on the custody record or in the interview record for action taken whilst an interview record is being kept, with a brief reference to this effect in the custody record.

12.12 Any decision to delay a break in an interview must be recorded, with reasons, in the interview record.

12.13 All written statements made at police stations under caution shall be written on forms provided for the purpose.

12.14 All written statements made under caution shall be taken in accordance with *Annex D*. Before a person makes a written statement under caution at a police station they shall be reminded about the right to legal advice. See *Note 12A*

C

Notes for guidance

12A *It is not normally necessary to ask for a written statement if the interview was recorded in writing and the record signed in accordance with paragraph 11.11 or audibly or visually recorded in accordance with Code E or F. Statements under caution should normally be taken in these circumstances only at the person's express wish. A person may however be asked if they want to make such a statement.*

12B *Meal breaks should normally last at least 15 minutes and shorter breaks after two hours should last at least 15 minutes. If the interviewer delays a break in accordance with paragraph 12.8 and prolongs the interview, a longer break should be provided. If there is a short interview, and another short interview is contemplated, the length of the break may be reduced if there are reasonable grounds to believe this is necessary to avoid any of the consequences in paragraph 12.8(i) to (iii).*

13   Interpreters

(a)   General

13.1 Chief officers are responsible for making sure appropriate arrangements are in place for provision of suitably qualified interpreters for people who:

* are deaf;

* do not understand English.

Whenever possible, interpreters should be drawn from the National Register of Public Service Interpreters (NRPSI) or the Council for the Advancement of Communication with Deaf People (CADCP) Directory of British Sign Language/English Interpreters.

(b)   Foreign languages

13.2 Unless *paragraphs 11.1, 11.18 to 11.20* apply, a person must not be interviewed in the absence of a person capable of interpreting if:

(a)   they have difficulty understanding English;

(b)   the interviewer cannot speak the person's own language;

C

(c)   the person wants an interpreter present.

13.3   The interviewer shall make sure the interpreter makes a note of the interview at the time in the person's language for use in the event of the interpreter being called to give evidence, and certifies its accuracy. The interviewer should allow sufficient time for the interpreter to note each question and answer after each is put, given and interpreted. The person should be allowed to read the record or have it read to them and sign it as correct or indicate the respects in which they consider it inaccurate. If the interview is audibly recorded or visually recorded, the arrangements in Code E or F apply.

13.4   In the case of a person making a statement to a police officer or other police staff other than in English:

(a)   the interpreter shall record the statement in the language it is made;

(b)   the person shall be invited to sign it;

(c)   an official English translation shall be made in due course.

(c)   Deaf people and people with speech difficulties

13.5   If a person appears to be deaf or there is doubt about their hearing or speaking ability, they must not be interviewed in the absence of an interpreter unless they agree in writing to being interviewed without one or *paragraphs 11.1, 11.18* to *11.20* apply.

13.6   An interpreter should also be called if a juvenile is interviewed and the parent or guardian present as the appropriate adult appears to be deaf or there is doubt about their hearing or speaking ability, unless they agree in writing to the interview proceeding without one or *paragraphs 11.1, 11.18* to *11.20* apply.

13.7   The interviewer shall make sure the interpreter is allowed to read the interview record and certify its accuracy in the event of the interpreter being called to give evidence. If the interview is audibly recorded or visually recorded, the arrangements in Code E or F apply.

(d)   Additional rules for detained persons

13.8   All reasonable attempts should be made to make the detainee understand that interpreters will be provided at public expense.

13.9   If *paragraph 6.1* applies and the detainee cannot communicate with the solicitor because of language, hearing or speech difficulties, an interpreter must be called. The interpreter may not be a police officer or any other police staff when interpretation is needed for the purposes of obtaining legal advice. In all other cases a police officer or other police staff may only interpret if the detainee and the appropriate adult, if applicable, give their agreement in writing or if the interview is audibly recorded or visually recorded as in Code E or F.

13.10 When the custody officer cannot establish effective communication with a person charged with an offence who appears deaf or there is doubt about their ability to hear, speak or to understand English, arrangements must be made as soon as practicable for an interpreter to explain the offence and any other information given by the custody officer.

(e)   Documentation

13.11 Action taken to call an interpreter under this section and any agreement to be interviewed in the absence of an interpreter must be recorded.

14   Questioning – special restrictions

14.1   If a person is arrested by one police force on behalf of another and the lawful period of detention in respect of that offence has not yet commenced in accordance with PACE, section 41 no questions may be put to them about the offence while they are in transit between the forces except to clarify any voluntary statement they make.

14.2   If a person is in police detention at a hospital they may not be questioned without the agreement of a responsible doctor. See *Note 14A*

Note for guidance

14A   If questioning takes place at a hospital under paragraph 14.2, or on the way to or from a hospital, the period of questioning concerned counts towards the total period of detention permitted.

15   Reviews and extensions of detention

(a)   Persons detained under PACE

15.1   The review officer is responsible under PACE, section 40 for periodically determining if a person's detention, before or after charge, continues to be necessary. This requirement continues throughout the detention period and except as in *paragraph 15.10*, the review officer must be present at the police station holding the detainee. See *Notes 15A* and *15B*

15.2   Under PACE, section 42, an officer of superintendent rank or above who is responsible for the station holding the detainee may give authority any time after the second review to extend the maximum period the person may be detained without charge by up to 12 hours. Further detention without charge may be authorised only by a magistrates' court in accordance with PACE, sections 43 and 44. See *Notes 15C, 15D* and *15E*

15.2A Section 42(1) of PACE as amended extends the maximum period of detention for indictable offences from 24 hours to 36 hours. Detaining a juvenile or mentally vulnerable person for longer than 24 hours will be dependent on the circumstances of the case and with regard to the person's:

(a)   special vulnerability;

(b)   the legal obligation to provide an opportunity for representations to be made prior to a decision about extending detention;

(c)   the need to consult and consider the views of any appropriate adult; and

(d)   any alternatives to police custody.

15.3   Before deciding whether to authorise continued detention the officer responsible under *paragraphs 15.1* or *15.2* shall give an opportunity to make representations about the detention to:

(a)   the detainee, unless in the case of a review as in *paragraph 15.1*, the detainee is asleep;

(b)   the detainee's solicitor if available at the time; and

(c)   the appropriate adult if available at the time.

15.3A Other people having an interest in the detainee's welfare may also make representations at the authorising officer's discretion.

15.3B Subject to *paragraph 15.10*, the representations may be made orally in person or by telephone or in writing. The authorising officer may, however, refuse to hear oral representations from the detainee if the officer considers them unfit to make representations because of their condition or behaviour. See *Note 15C*

15.3C The decision on whether the review takes place in person or by telephone or by video conferencing (see Note 15G) is a matter for the review officer. In determining the form the review may take, the review officer must always take full account of the needs of the person in custody. The benefits of carrying out a review in person should always be considered, based on the individual circumstances of each case with specific additional consideration if the person is:

(a)   a juvenile (and the age of the juvenile); or

(b)   mentally vulnerable; or

(c)   has been subject to medical attention for other than routine minor ailments; or

(d)   there are presentational or community issues around the person's detention.

15.4   Before conducting a review or determining whether to extend the maximum period of detention without charge, the officer responsible must make sure the detainee is reminded of their entitlement to free legal advice, see *paragraph 6.5,* unless in the case of a review the person is asleep.

15.5   If, after considering any representations, the officer decides to keep the detainee in detention or extend the maximum period they may be detained without charge, any comment made by the detainee shall be recorded. If applicable, the officer responsible under *paragraph 15.1* or *15.2* shall be informed of the comment as soon as practicable. See also *paragraphs 11.4* and *11.13*

15.6   No officer shall put specific questions to the detainee:

•   regarding their involvement in any offence; or

•   in respect of any comments they may make:

    −   when given the opportunity to make representations; or

    −   in response to a decision to keep them in detention or extend the maximum period of detention.

Such an exchange could constitute an interview as in *paragraph 11.1A* and would be subject to the associated safeguards in *section 11* and, in respect of a person who has been charged, *paragraph 16.5.* See also *paragraph 11.13*

15.7   A detainee who is asleep at a review, see *paragraph 15.1,* and whose continued detention is authorised must be informed about the decision and reason as soon as practicable after waking.

15.8   Not used

(b)   *Telephone review of detention*

15.9   PACE, section 40A provides that the officer responsible under section 40 for reviewing the detention of a person who has not been charged, need not attend the police station holding the detainee and may carry out the review by telephone.

15.9A PACE, section 45A(2) provides that the officer responsible under section 40 for reviewing the detention of a person who has not been charged, need not attend the police station holding the detainee and may carry out the review by video conferencing facilities (See *Note 15G*).

15.9B A telephone review is not permitted where facilities for review by video conferencing exist and it is practicable to use them.

15.9C The review officer can decide at any stage that a telephone review or review by video conferencing should be terminated and that the review will be conducted in person. The reasons for doing so should be noted in the custody record.

See *Note 15F*

15.10 When a telephone review is carried out, an officer at the station holding the detainee shall be required by the review officer to fulfil that officer's obligations under PACE section 40 or this Code by:

(a)   making any record connected with the review in the detainee's custody record;

(b)   if applicable, making a record in (a) in the presence of the detainee; and

(c)   giving the detainee information about the review.

15.11 When a telephone review is carried out, the requirement in *paragraph 15.3* will be satisfied:

(a)   if facilities exist for the immediate transmission of written representations to the review officer, e.g. fax or email message, by giving the detainee an opportunity to make representations:

(i)   orally by telephone; or

(ii)   in writing using those facilities; and

(b)   in all other cases, by giving the detainee an opportunity to make their representations orally by telephone.

(c)   Documentation

15.12 It is the officer's responsibility to make sure all reminders given under *paragraph 15.4* are noted in the custody record.

15.13 The grounds for, and extent of, any delay in conducting a review shall be recorded.

15.14 When a telephone review is carried out, a record shall be made of:

(a)   the reason the review officer did not attend the station holding the detainee;

(b)   the place the review officer was;

(c)   the method representations, oral or written, were made to the review officer, see *paragraph 15.11*.

15.15 Any written representations shall be retained.

15.16 A record shall be made as soon as practicable about the outcome of each review or determination whether to extend the maximum detention period without charge or an application for a warrant of further detention or its extension. If *paragraph 15.7* applies, a record shall also be made of when the person was informed and by whom. If an authorisation is given under PACE, section 42, the record shall state the number of hours and minutes by which the detention period is extended or further extended. If a warrant for further detention, or extension, is granted under section 43 or 44, the record shall state the detention period authorised by the warrant and the date and time it was granted.

C

Notes for guidance

15A   Review officer for the purposes of:

- PACE, sections 40 and 40A means, in the case of a person arrested but not charged, an officer of at least inspector rank not directly involved in the investigation and, if a person has been arrested and charged, the custody officer;

15B   The detention of persons in police custody not subject to the statutory review requirement in paragraph 15.1 should still be reviewed periodically as a matter of good practice. Such reviews can be carried out by an officer of the rank of sergeant or above. The purpose of such reviews is to check the particular power under which a detainee is held continues to apply, any associated conditions are complied with and to make sure appropriate action is taken to deal with any changes. This includes the detainee's prompt release when the power no longer applies, or their transfer if the power requires the detainee be taken elsewhere as soon as the necessary arrangements are made. Examples include persons:

(a)   arrested on warrant because they failed to answer bail to appear at court;

(b)   arrested under the Bail Act 1976, section 7(3) for breaching a condition of bail granted after charge;

(c)   in police custody for specific purposes and periods under the Crime (Sentences) Act 1997, Schedule 1;

(d)   convicted, or remand prisoners, held in police stations on behalf of the Prison Service under the Imprisonment (Temporary Provisions) Act 1980, section 6;

C

(e)   *being detained to prevent them causing a breach of the peace;*

(f)   *detained at police stations on behalf of the Immigration Service.*

(g)   *detained by order of a magistrates' court under the Criminal Justice Act 1988, section 152 (as amended by the Drugs Act 2005, section 8) to facilitate the recovery of evidence after being charged with drug possession or drug trafficking and suspected of having swallowed drugs.*

The detention of persons remanded into police detention by order of a court under the Magistrates' Courts Act 1980, section 128 is subject to a statutory requirement to review that detention. This is to make sure the detainee is taken back to court no later than the end of the period authorised by the court or when the need for their detention by police ceases, whichever is the sooner.

15C   *In the case of a review of detention, but not an extension, the detainee need not be woken for the review. However, if the detainee is likely to be asleep, e.g. during a period of rest allowed as in paragraph 12.2, at the latest time a review or authorisation to extend detention may take place, the officer should, if the legal obligations and time constraints permit, bring forward the procedure to allow the detainee to make representations. A detainee not asleep during the review must be present when the grounds for their continued detention are recorded and must at the same time be informed of those grounds unless the review officer considers the person is incapable of understanding what is said, violent or likely to become violent or in urgent need of medical attention.*

15D   *An application to a Magistrates' Court under PACE, sections 43 or 44 for a warrant of further detention or its extension should be made between 10am and 9pm, and if possible during normal court hours. It will not usually be practicable to arrange for a court to sit specially outside the hours of 10am to 9pm. If it appears a special sitting may be needed outside normal court hours but between 10am and 9pm, the clerk to the justices should be given notice and informed of this possibility, while the court is sitting if possible.*

15E   *In paragraph 15.2, the officer responsible for the station holding the detainee includes a superintendent or above who, in accordance with their force operational policy or police regulations, is given that responsibility on a temporary basis whilst the appointed long-term holder is off duty or otherwise unavailable.*

15F   *The provisions of PACE, section 40A allowing telephone reviews do not apply to reviews of detention after charge by the custody officer When video conferencing is not required, they allow the use of a telephone to carry out a review of detention before charge. The procedure under PACE, section 42 must be done in person.*

15G   *The use of video conferencing facilities for decisions about detention under section 45A of PACE is subject to the introduction of regulations by the Secretary of State.*

16   Charging detained persons

(a)   *Action*

16.1   When the officer in charge of the investigation reasonably believes there is sufficient evidence to provide a realistic prospect of conviction for the offence (see *paragraph 11.6)*, they shall without delay, and subject to the following qualification, inform the custody officer who will be responsible for considering whether the detainee should be charged. See *Notes 11B* and *16A*. When a person is detained in respect of more than one offence it is permissible to delay informing the custody officer until the above conditions are satisfied in respect of all the offences, but see *paragraph 11.6*. If the detainee is a juvenile, mentally disordered or otherwise mentally vulnerable, any resulting action shall be taken in the presence of the appropriate adult if they are present at the time. See *Notes 16B* and *16C*

16.1A Where guidance issued by the Director of Public Prosecutions under section 37A is in force the custody officer must comply with that Guidance in deciding how to act in dealing with the detainee. See *Notes 16AA* and *16AB*.

16.1B Where in compliance with the DPP's Guidance the custody officer decides that the case should be immediately referred to the CPS to make the charging decision, consultation should take place with a Crown Prosecutor as soon as is reasonably practicable. Where the Crown Prosecutor is unable to make the charging decision on the information available at that time, the detainee may be released without charge and on bail (with conditions if necessary) under section 37(7)(a). In such circumstances, the detainee should be informed that they are being released to enable the Director of Public Prosecutions to make a decision under section 37B.

16.2   When a detainee is charged with or informed they may be prosecuted for an offence, see *Note 16B,* they shall, unless the restriction on drawing adverse inferences from silence applies, see *Annex C,* be cautioned as follows:

> *'You do not have to say anything. But it may harm your defence if you do not mention now something which you later rely on in court. Anything you do say may be given in evidence.'*

Annex C, paragraph 2 sets out the alternative terms of the caution to be used when the restriction on drawing adverse inferences from silence applies.

16.3 When a detainee is charged they shall be given a written notice showing particulars of the offence and, subject to *paragraph 2.6A*, the officer's name and the case reference number. As far as possible the particulars of the charge shall be stated in simple terms, but they shall also show the precise offence in law with which the detainee is charged. The notice shall begin:

> *'You are charged with the offence(s) shown below.'* Followed by the caution.

If the detainee is a juvenile, mentally disordered or otherwise mentally vulnerable, the notice should be given to the appropriate adult.

16.4 If, after a detainee has been charged with or informed they may be prosecuted for an offence, an officer wants to tell them about any written statement or interview with another person relating to such an offence, the detainee shall either be handed a true copy of the written statement or the content of the interview record brought to their attention. Nothing shall be done to invite any reply or comment except to:

(a) caution the detainee, *'You do not have to say anything, but anything you do say may be given in evidence.'*; and

(b) remind the detainee about their right to legal advice.

16.4A If the detainee:

- cannot read, the document may be read to them

- is a juvenile, mentally disordered or otherwise mentally vulnerable, the appropriate adult shall also be given a copy, or the interview record shall be brought to their attention

16.5 A detainee may not be interviewed about an offence after they have been charged with, or informed they may be prosecuted for it, unless the interview is necessary:

- to prevent or minimise harm or loss to some other person, or the public

- to clear up an ambiguity in a previous answer or statement

- in the interests of justice for the detainee to have put to them, and have an opportunity to comment on, information concerning the offence which has come to light since they were charged or informed they might be prosecuted

Before any such interview, the interviewer shall:

(a) caution the detainee, *'You do not have to say anything, but anything you do say may be given in evidence.'*;

(b) remind the detainee about their right to legal advice.

See *Note 16B*

16.6 The provisions of *paragraphs 16.2* to *16.5* must be complied with in the appropriate adult's presence if they are already at the police station. If they are not at the police station then these provisions must be complied with again in their presence when they arrive unless the detainee has been released.

See *Note 16C*

16.7 When a juvenile is charged with an offence and the custody officer authorises their continued detention after charge, the custody officer must try to make arrangements for the juvenile to be taken into the care of a local authority to be detained pending appearance in court unless the custody officer certifies it is impracticable to do so or, in the case of a juvenile of at least 12 years old, no secure accommodation is available and there is a risk to the public of serious harm from that juvenile, in accordance with PACE, section 38(6). See *Note 16D*

(b)   Documentation

16.8 A record shall be made of anything a detainee says when charged.

16.9 Any questions put in an interview after charge and answers given relating to the offence shall be recorded in full during the interview on forms for that purpose and the record signed by the detainee or, if they refuse, by the interviewer and any third parties present. If the questions are audibly recorded or visually recorded the arrangements in Code E or F apply.

16.10 If it is not practicable to make arrangements for a juvenile's transfer into local authority care as in *paragraph 16.7,* the custody officer must record the reasons and complete a certificate to be produced before the court with the juvenile. See *Note 16D*

Notes for guidance

16A   The custody officer must take into account alternatives to prosecution under the Crime and Disorder Act 1998, reprimands and warning applicable to persons under 18, and in national guidance on the cautioning of offenders, for persons aged 18 and over.

16AA   When a person is arrested under the provisions of the Criminal Justice Act 2003 which allow a person to be re-tried after being acquitted of a serious offence which is a qualifying offence specified in Schedule 5 to that Act and not precluded from further prosecution by virtue of section 75(3) of that Act the detention provisions of PACE are modified and make an officer of the rank of superintendent or above who has not been

C

directly involved in the investigation responsible for determining whether the evidence is sufficient to charge.

16AB Where Guidance issued by the Director of Public Prosecutions under section 37B is in force, a custody officer who determines in accordance with that Guidance that there is sufficient evidence to charge the detainee, may detain that person for no longer than is reasonably necessary to decide how that person is to be dealt with under PACE, section 37(7)(a) to (d), including, where appropriate, consultation with the Duty Prosecutor. The period is subject to the maximum period of detention before charge determined by PACE, sections 41 to 44. Where in accordance with the Guidance the case is referred to the CPS for decision, the custody officer should ensure that an officer involved in the investigation sends to the CPS such information as is specified in the Guidance.

16B The giving of a warning or the service of the Notice of Intended Prosecution required by the Road Traffic Offenders Act 1988, section 1 does not amount to informing a detainee they may be prosecuted for an offence and so does not preclude further questioning in relation to that offence.

16C There is no power under PACE to detain a person and delay action under paragraphs 16.2 to 16.5 solely to await the arrival of the appropriate adult. After charge, bail cannot be refused, or release on bail delayed, simply because an appropriate adult is not available, unless the absence of that adult provides the custody officer with the necessary grounds to authorise detention after charge under PACE, section 38.

16D Except as in paragraph 16.7, neither a juvenile's behaviour nor the nature of the offence provides grounds for the custody officer to decide it is impracticable to arrange the juvenile's transfer to local authority care. Similarly, the lack of secure local authority accommodation does not make it impracticable to transfer the juvenile. The availability of secure accommodation is only a factor in relation to a juvenile aged 12 or over when the local authority accommodation would not be adequate to protect the public from serious harm from them. The obligation to transfer a juvenile to local authority accommodation applies as much to a juvenile charged during the daytime as to a juvenile to be held overnight, subject to a requirement to bring the juvenile before a court under PACE, section 46.

17 Testing persons for the presence of specified Class A drugs

(a) Action

17.1 This section of Code C applies only in selected police stations in police areas where the provisions for drug testing under section 63B of PACE (as amended by section 5 of the Criminal Justice Act 2003 and section 7 of the Drugs Act 2005) are in force and

54

in respect of which the Secretary of State has given a notification to the relevant chief officer of police that arrangements for the taking of samples have been made. Such a notification will cover either a police area as a whole or particular stations within a police area. The notification indicates whether the testing applies to those arrested or charged or under the age of 18 as the case may be and testing can only take place in respect of the persons so indicated in the notification. Testing cannot be carried out unless the relevant notification has been given and has not been withdrawn. See *Note 17F*

C

17.2　A sample of urine or a non-intimate sample may be taken from a person in police detention for the purpose of ascertaining whether he has any specified Class A drug in his body only where they have been brought before the custody officer and:

(a)　either the arrest condition, see *paragraph 17.3*, or the charge condition, see *paragraph 17.4* is met;

(h)　the age condition see *paragraph 17.5*, is met;

(c)　the notification condition is met in relation to the arrest condition, the charge condition, or the age condition, as the case may be. (Testing on charge and/or arrest must be specifically provided for in the notification for the power to apply. In addition, the fact that testing of under 18s is authorised must be expressly provided for in the notification before the power to test such persons applies.). See *paragraph 17.1*; and

(d)　a police officer has requested the person concerned to give the sample (the request condition).

17.3　The arrest condition is met where the detainee:

(a)　has been arrested for a trigger offence, see *Note 17E*, but not charged with that offence; or

(b)　has been arrested for any other offence but not charged with that offence and a police officer of inspector rank or above, who has reasonable grounds for suspecting that their misuse of any specified Class A drug caused or contributed to the offence, has authorised the sample to be taken.

17.4　The charge condition is met where the detainee:

(a)　has been charged with a trigger offence, or

(b)　has been charged with any other offence and a police officer of inspector rank or above, who has reasonable grounds for suspecting that the detainee's misuse of any specified Class A drug caused or contributed to the offence, has authorised the sample to be taken.

17.5 The age condition is met where:

    (a)   in the case of a detainee who has been arrested but not charged as in *paragraph 17.3*, they are aged 18 or over;

    (b)   in the case of a detainee who has been charged as in *paragraph 17.4*, they are aged 14 or over.

17.6 Before requesting a sample from the person concerned, an officer must:

    (a)   inform them that the purpose of taking the sample is for drug testing under PACE. This is to ascertain whether they have a specified Class A drug present in their body;

    (b)   warn them that if, when so requested, they fail without good cause to provide a sample they may be liable to prosecution;

    (c)   where the taking of the sample has been authorised by an inspector or above in accordance with *paragraph 17.3(b)* or *17.4(b)* above, inform them that the authorisation has been given and the grounds for giving it;

    (d)   remind them of the following rights, which may be exercised at any stage during the period in custody:

        (i)   the right to have someone informed of their arrest [see section 5];

        (ii)   the right to consult privately with a solicitor and that free independent legal advice is available [see section 6]; and

        (iii)   the right to consult these Codes of Practice [see section 3].

17.7 In the case of a person who has not attained the age of 17 —

    (a)   the making of the request for a sample under *paragraph 17.2(d)* above;

    (b)   the giving of the warning and the information under *paragraph 17.6* above; and

    (c)   the taking of the sample,

may not take place except in the presence of an appropriate adult. (see Note 17G)

17.8 Authorisation by an officer of the rank of inspector or above within *paragraph 17.3(b)* or *17.4(b)* may be given orally or in writing but, if it is given orally, it must be confirmed in writing as soon as practicable.

17.9 If a sample is taken from a detainee who has been arrested for an offence but not charged with that offence as in *paragraph 17.3*, no further sample may be taken during the same continuous period of detention. If during that same period the charge condition is also met in respect of that detainee, the sample which has been taken shall be treated as being taken by virtue of the charge condition, see *paragraph 17.4*, being met.

17.10 A detainee from whom a sample may be taken may be detained for up to six hours from the time of charge if the custody officer reasonably believes the detention is necessary to enable a sample to be taken. Where the arrest condition is met, a detainee whom the custody officer has decided to release on bail without charge may continue to be detained, but not beyond 24 hours from the relevant time (as defined in section 41(2) of PACE), to enable a sample to be taken.

17.11 A detainee in respect of whom the arrest condition is met, but not the charge condition, see *paragraphs 17.3* and *17.4*, and whose release would be required before a sample can be taken had they not continued to be detained as a result of being arrested for a further offence which does not satisfy the arrest condition, may have a sample taken at any time within 24 hours after the arrest for the offence that satisfies the arrest condition.

(b)   Documentation

17.12 The following must be recorded in the custody record:

    (a)   if a sample is taken following authorisation by an officer of the rank of inspector or above, the authorisation and the grounds for suspicion;

    (b)   the giving of a warning of the consequences of failure to provide a sample;

    (c)   the time at which the sample was given; and

    (d)   the time of charge or, where the arrest condition is being relied upon, the time of arrest and, where applicable, the fact that a sample taken after arrest but before charge is to be treated as being taken by virtue of the charge condition, where that is met in the same period of continuous detention. See *paragraph 17.9*

(c)   General

17.13 A sample may only be taken by a prescribed person. See *Note 17C*.

17.14 Force may not be used to take any sample for the purpose of drug testing.

17.15 The terms "Class A drug" and "misuse" have the same meanings as in the Misuse of Drugs Act 1971. "Specified" (in relation to a Class A drug) and "trigger offence" have the same meanings as in Part III of the Criminal Justice and Court Services Act 2000.

17.16 Any sample taken:

(a) may not be used for any purpose other than to ascertain whether the person concerned has a specified Class A drug present in his body; and

(b) must be retained until the person concerned has made their first appearance before the court.

C

(d) Assessment of misuse of drugs

17.17 Under the provisions of Part 3 of the Drugs Act 2005, where a detainee has tested positive for a specified Class A drug under section 63B of PACE a police officer may, at any time before the person's release from the police station, impose a requirement for them to attend an initial assessment of their drug misuse by a suitably qualified person and to remain for its duration. The requirement may only be imposed on a person if:

(a) they have reached the age of 18

(b) notification has been given by the Secretary of State to the relevant chief officer of police that arrangements for conducting initial assessments have been made for those from whom samples for testing have been taken at the police station where the detainee is in custody.

17.18 When imposing a requirement to attend an initial assessment the police officer must:

(a) inform the person of the time and place at which the initial assessment is to take place;

(b) explain that this information will be confirmed in writing; and

(c) warn the person that he may be liable to prosecution if he fails without good cause to attend the initial assessment and remain for it's duration

17.19 Where a police officer has imposed a requirement to attend an initial assessment in accordance with *paragraph 17.17*, he must, before the person is released from detention, give the person notice in writing which:

(a) confirms that he is required to attend and remain for the duration of an initial assessment; and

(b) confirms the information and repeats the warning referred to in *paragraph 17.18*.

17.20 The following must be recorded in the custody record:

(a) that the requirement to attend an initial assessment has been imposed; and

(b)   the information, explanation, warning and notice given in accordance with *paragraphs 17.17* and *17.19*.

17.21 Where a notice is given in accordance with *paragraph 17.19*, a police officer can give the person a further notice in writing which informs the person of any change to the time or place at which the initial assessment is to take place and which repeats the warning referred to in *paragraph 17.18(c)*.

17.22 Part 3 of the Drugs Act 2005 also requires police officers to have regard to any guidance issued by the Secretary of State in respect of the assessment provisions.

C

Notes for guidance

17A   When warning a person who is asked to provide a urine or non-intimate sample in accordance with paragraph 17.6(b), the following form of words may be used:

"You do not have to provide a sample, but I must warn you that if you fail or refuse without good cause to do so, you will commit an offence for which you may be imprisoned, or fined, or both".

17B   A sample has to be sufficient and suitable. A sufficient sample is sufficient in quantity and quality to enable drug-testing analysis to take place. A suitable sample is one which by its nature, is suitable for a particular form of drug analysis.

17C   A prescribed person in paragraph 17.13 is one who is prescribed in regulations made by the Secretary of State under section 63B(6) of the Police and Criminal Evidence Act 1984. [The regulations are currently contained in regulation SI 2001 No. 2645, the Police and Criminal Evidence Act 1984 (Drug Testing Persons in Police Detention) (Prescribed Persons) Regulations 2001.]

17D   The retention of the sample in paragraph 17.16(b) allows for the sample to be sent for confirmatory testing and analysis if the detainee disputes the test. But such samples, and the information derived from them, may not be subsequently used in the investigation of any offence or in evidence against the persons from whom they were taken.

17E   Trigger offences are:

1.   Offences under the following provisions of the Theft Act 1968:

section 1	*(theft)*
section 8	*(robbery)*
section 9	*(burglary)*
section 10	*(aggravated burglary)*

C

section 12   *(taking a motor vehicle or other conveyance without authority)*

section 12A   *(aggravated vehicle-taking)*

section 15   *(obtaining property by deception)*

section 22   *(handling stolen goods)*

section 25   *(going equipped for stealing etc.)*

2.   *Offences under the following provisions of the Misuse of Drugs Act 1971, if committed in respect of a specified Class A drug:–*

section 4   *(restriction on production and supply of controlled drugs)*

section 5(2)   *(possession of a controlled drug)*

section 5(3)   *(possession of a controlled drug with intent to supply)*

3.   *An offence under section 1(1) of the Criminal Attempts Act 1981 if committed in respect of an offence under any of the following provisions of the Theft Act 1968:*

section 1   *(theft)*

section 8   *(robbery)*

section 9   *(burglary)*

section 15   *(obtaining property by deception)*

section 22   *(handling stolen goods)*

4.   *Offences under the following provisions of the Vagrancy Act 1824:*

section 3   *(begging)*

section 4   *(persistent begging)*

17F   *The power to take samples is subject to notification by the Secretary of State that appropriate arrangements for the taking of samples have been made for the police area as a whole or for the particular police station concerned for whichever of the following is specified in the notification:*

(a)   *persons in respect of whom the arrest condition is met;*

(b)   *persons in respect of whom the charge condition is met;*

(c)   *persons who have not attained the age of 18.*

Note: Notification is treated as having been given for the purposes of the charge condition in relation to a police area, if testing (on charge) under section 63B(2) of PACE was in force immediately before section 7 of the Drugs Act 2005 was brought into force; and for the purposes of the age condition, in relation to a police area or police station, if immediately before that day, notification that arrangements had been made for the taking of samples from persons under the age of 18 (those aged 14-17) had been given and had not been withdrawn.

17G   Appropriate adult in paragraph 17.7 means the person's –

(a)   parent or guardian or, if they are in the care of a local authority or voluntary organisation, a person representing that authority or organisation; or

(b)   a social worker of, in England, a local authority or, in Wales, a local authority social services department; or

(c)   if no person falling within (a) or (b) above is available, any responsible person aged 18 or over who is not a police officer or a person employed by the police.

ANNEX A – INTIMATE AND STRIP SEARCHES

A **Intimate search**

1. An intimate search consists of the physical examination of a person's body orifices other than the mouth. The intrusive nature of such searches means the actual and potential risks associated with intimate searches must never be underestimated.

(a) *Action*

2. Body orifices other than the mouth may be searched only:

   (a) if authorised by an officer of inspector rank or above who has reasonable grounds for believing that the person may have concealed on themselves:

   (i) anything which they could and might use to cause physical injury to themselves or others at the station; or

   (ii) a Class A drug which they intended to supply to another or to export;

   and the officer has reasonable grounds for believing that an intimate search is the only means of removing those items; and

   (b) if the search is under *paragraph 2(a)(ii)* (a drug offence search), the detainee's appropriate consent has been given in writing.

2A. Before the search begins, a police officer, designated detention officer or staff custody officer, must tell the detainee:-

   (a) that the authority to carry out the search has been given;

   (b) the grounds for giving the authorisation and for believing that the article cannot be removed without an intimate search.

2B Before a detainee is asked to give appropriate consent to a search under *paragraph 2(a)(ii)* (a drug offence search) they must be warned that if they refuse without good cause their refusal may harm their case if it comes to trial, see *Note A6*. This warning may be given by a police officer or member of police staff. A detainee who is not legally represented must be reminded of their entitlement to have free legal advice, see Code C, *paragraph 6.5*, and the reminder noted in the custody record.

3. An intimate search may only be carried out by a registered medical practitioner or registered nurse, unless an officer of at least inspector rank considers this is not practicable and the search is to take place under *paragraph 2(a)(i)*, in which case a police officer may carry out the search. See *Notes A1 to A5*

3A. Any proposal for a search under *paragraph 2(a)(i)* to be carried out by someone other than a registered medical practitioner or registered nurse must only be considered as a last resort and when the authorising officer is satisfied the risks associated with allowing the item to remain with the detainee outweigh the risks associated with removing it. See *Notes A1 to A5*

4.   An intimate search under:

 •   *paragraph 2(a)(i)* may take place only at a hospital, surgery, other medical premises or police station

 •   *paragraph 2(a)(ii)* may take place only at a hospital, surgery or other medical premises and must be carried out by a registered medical practitioner or a registered nurse

5.   An intimate search at a police station of a juvenile or mentally disordered or otherwise mentally vulnerable person may take place only in the presence of an appropriate adult of the same sex, unless the detainee specifically requests a particular adult of the opposite sex who is readily available. In the case of a juvenile the search may take place in the absence of the appropriate adult only if the juvenile signifies in the presence of the appropriate adult they do not want the adult present during the search and the adult agrees. A record shall be made of the juvenile's decision and signed by the appropriate adult.

6.   When an intimate search under *paragraph 2(a)(i)* is carried out by a police officer, the officer must be of the same sex as the detainee. A minimum of two people, other than the detainee, must be present during the search. Subject to *paragraph 5*, no person of the opposite sex who is not a medical practitioner or nurse shall be present, nor shall anyone whose presence is unnecessary. The search shall be conducted with proper regard to the sensitivity and vulnerability of the detainee.

(b)   Documentation

7.   In the case of an intimate search, the following shall be recorded as soon as practicable, in the detainee's custody record:

 (a) for searches under *paragraphs 2(a)(i)* and *(ii)*;

  •   the authorisation to carry out the search;

  •   the grounds for giving the authorisation;

  •   the grounds for believing the article could not be removed without an intimate search

C

- which parts of the detainee's body were searched

- who carried out the search

- who was present

- the result.

(b) for searches under paragraph 2(a)(ii):

- the giving of the warning required by *paragraph 2B*;

- the fact that the appropriate consent was given or (as the case may be) refused, and if refused, the reason given for the refusal (if any).

8. If an intimate search is carried out by a police officer, the reason why it was impracticable for a registered medical practitioner or registered nurse to conduct it must be recorded.

B   Strip search

9. A strip search is a search involving the removal of more than outer clothing. In this Code, outer clothing includes shoes and socks.

(a)   Action

10. A strip search may take place only if it is considered necessary to remove an article which a detainee would not be allowed to keep, and the officer reasonably considers the detainee might have concealed such an article. Strip searches shall not be routinely carried out if there is no reason to consider that articles are concealed.

The conduct of strip searches

11. When strip searches are conducted:

(a) a police officer carrying out a strip search must be the same sex as the detainee;

(b) the search shall take place in an area where the detainee cannot be seen by anyone who does not need to be present, nor by a member of the opposite sex except an appropriate adult who has been specifically requested by the detainee;

(c) except in cases of urgency, where there is risk of serious harm to the detainee or to others, whenever a strip search involves exposure of intimate body parts, there must be at least two people present other than the detainee, and if the search is of a juvenile or mentally disordered or otherwise mentally vulnerable person, one of the people must be the appropriate adult. Except in urgent cases as above, a search of a juvenile may take place in the absence of the appropriate adult only if the juvenile signifies in the presence of the appropriate adult that they do not want the adult to be present during the search and the adult agrees. A record shall be made of the juvenile's decision and signed by the appropriate adult. The presence of more than two people, other than an appropriate adult, shall be permitted only in the most exceptional circumstances;

(d) the search shall be conducted with proper regard to the sensitivity and vulnerability of the detainee in these circumstances and every reasonable effort shall be made to secure the detainee's co-operation and minimise embarrassment. Detainees who are searched shall not normally be required to remove all their clothes at the same time, e.g. a person should be allowed to remove clothing above the waist and redress before removing further clothing;

(e) If necessary to assist the search, the detainee may be required to hold their arms in the air or to stand with their legs apart and bend forward so a visual examination may be made of the genital and anal areas provided no physical contact is made with any body orifice;

(f) if articles are found, the detainee shall be asked to hand them over. If articles are found within any body orifice other than the mouth, and the detainee refuses to hand them over, their removal would constitute an intimate search, which must be carried out as in *Part A*;

(g) a strip search shall be conducted as quickly as possible, and the detainee allowed to dress as soon as the procedure is complete.

(b) Documentation

12. A record shall be made on the custody record of a strip search including the reason it was considered necessary, those present and any result.

Notes for guidance

A1 *Before authorising any intimate search, the authorising officer must make every reasonable effort to persuade the detainee to hand the article over without a search. If the detainee agrees, a registered medical practitioner or registered nurse should whenever possible be asked to assess the risks involved and, if necessary, attend to assist the detainee.*

A2 *If the detainee does not agree to hand the article over without a search, the authorising officer must carefully review all the relevant factors before authorising an intimate search.*

In particular, the officer must consider whether the grounds for believing an article may be concealed are reasonable.

A3 *If authority is given for a search under paragraph 2(a)(i), a registered medical practitioner or registered nurse shall be consulted whenever possible. The presumption should be that the search will be conducted by the registered medical practitioner or registered nurse and the authorising officer must make every reasonable effort to persuade the detainee to allow the medical practitioner or nurse to conduct the search.*

A4 *A constable should only be authorised to carry out a search as a last resort and when all other approaches have failed. In these circumstances, the authorising officer must be satisfied the detainee might use the article for one or more of the purposes in paragraph 2(a)(i) and the physical injury likely to be caused is sufficiently severe to justify authorising a constable to carry out the search.*

A5 *If an officer has any doubts whether to authorise an intimate search by a constable, the officer should seek advice from an officer of superintendent rank or above.*

A6 *In warning a detainee who is asked to consent to an intimate drug offence search, as in paragraph 2B, the following form of words may be used:*

"You do not have to allow yourself to be searched, but I must warn you that if you refuse without good cause, your refusal may harm your case if it comes to trial."

ANNEX B – DELAY IN NOTIFYING ARREST OR ALLOWING ACCESS TO LEGAL ADVICE

A   Persons detained under PACE

1.   The exercise of the rights in *Section 5* or *Section 6,* or both, may be delayed if the person is in police detention, as in PACE, section 118(2), in connection with an indictable offence, has not yet been charged with an offence and an officer of superintendent rank or above, or inspector rank or above only for the rights in *Section 5*, has reasonable grounds for believing their exercise will:

(i)   lead to:

- interference with, or harm to, evidence connected with an indictable offence; or

- interference with, or physical harm to, other people; or

(ii)   lead to alerting other people suspected of having committed an indictable offence but not yet arrested for it; or

(iii)   hinder the recovery of property obtained in consequence of the commission of such an offence.

2.   These rights may also be delayed if the officer has reasonable grounds to believe that:

(i)   the person detained for an indictable offence has benefited from their criminal conduct (decided in accordance with Part 2 of the Proceeds of Crime Act 2002); and

(ii)   the recovery of the value of the property constituting that benefit will be hindered by the exercise of either right.

3.   Authority to delay a detainee's right to consult privately with a solicitor may be given only if the authorising officer has reasonable grounds to believe the solicitor the detainee wants to consult will, inadvertently or otherwise, pass on a message from the detainee or act in some other way which will have any of the consequences specified under *paragraphs 1 or 2*. In these circumstances the detainee must be allowed to choose another solicitor. See *Note B3*

4.   If the detainee wishes to see a solicitor, access to that solicitor may not be delayed on the grounds they might advise the detainee not to answer questions or the solicitor was initially asked to attend the police station by someone else. In the latter case the detainee must be told the solicitor has come to the police station at another person's request, and must be asked to sign the custody record to signify whether they want to see the solicitor.

C

5.   The fact the grounds for delaying notification of arrest may be satisfied does not automatically mean the grounds for delaying access to legal advice will also be satisfied.

6.   These rights may be delayed only for as long as grounds exist and in no case beyond 36 hours after the relevant time as in PACE, section 41. If the grounds cease to apply within this time, the detainee must, as soon as practicable, be asked if they want to exercise either right, the custody record must be noted accordingly, and action taken in accordance with the relevant section of the Code.

7.   A detained person must be permitted to consult a solicitor for a reasonable time before any court hearing.

B   Not used

C   Documentation

13.   The grounds for action under this Annex shall be recorded and the detainee informed of them as soon as practicable.

14.   Any reply given by a detainee under *paragraphs 6* or *11* must be recorded and the detainee asked to endorse the record in relation to whether they want to receive legal advice at this point.

D   Cautions and special warnings

15.   When a suspect detained at a police station is interviewed during any period for which access to legal advice has been delayed under this Annex, the court or jury may not draw adverse inferences from their silence.

Notes for guidance

B1   Even if Annex B applies in the case of a juvenile, or a person who is mentally disordered or otherwise mentally vulnerable, action to inform the appropriate adult and the person responsible for a juvenile's welfare if that is a different person, must nevertheless be taken as in paragraph 3.13 and 3.15.

B2   In the case of Commonwealth citizens and foreign nationals, see Note 7A.

B3   A decision to delay access to a specific solicitor is likely to be a rare occurrence and only when it can be shown the suspect is capable of misleading that particular solicitor and there is more than a substantial risk that the suspect will succeed in causing information to be conveyed which will lead to one or more of the specified consequences.

ANNEX C – RESTRICTION ON DRAWING ADVERSE INFERENCES FROM SILENCE AND TERMS OF THE CAUTION WHEN THE RESTRICTION APPLIES

(a) *The restriction on drawing adverse inferences from silence*

1. The Criminal Justice and Public Order Act 1994, sections 34, 36 and 37 as amended by the Youth Justice and Criminal Evidence Act 1999, section 58 describe the conditions under which adverse inferences may be drawn from a person's failure or refusal to say anything about their involvement in the offence when interviewed, after being charged or informed they may be prosecuted. These provisions are subject to an overriding restriction on the ability of a court or jury to draw adverse inferences from a person's silence. This restriction applies:

    (a) to any detainee at a police station, see Note 10C who, before being interviewed, see *section 11* or being charged or informed they may be prosecuted, see section 16, has:

        (i) asked for legal advice, see *section 6, paragraph 6.1*;

        (ii) not been allowed an opportunity to consult a solicitor, including the duty solicitor, as in this Code; and

        (iii) not changed their mind about wanting legal advice, see *section 6, paragraph 6.6(d)*

        Note the condition in (ii) will

            – apply when a detainee who has asked for legal advice is interviewed before speaking to a solicitor as in *section 6, paragraph 6.6(a)* or *(b)*.

            – not apply if the detained person declines to ask for the duty solicitor, see *section 6, paragraphs 6.6(c)* and *(d)*;

    (b) to any person charged with, or informed they may be prosecuted for, an offence who:

        (i) has had brought to their notice a written statement made by another person or the content of an interview with another person which relates to that offence, see *section 16, paragraph 16.4*;

        (ii) is interviewed about that offence, see *section 16, paragraph 16.5*; or

        (iii) makes a written statement about that offence, see *Annex D paragraphs 4* and *9*.

(b)   Terms of the caution when the restriction applies

2.   When a requirement to caution arises at a time when the restriction on drawing adverse inferences from silence applies, the caution shall be:

'You do not have to say anything, but anything you do say may be given in evidence.'

C

3.   Whenever the restriction either begins to apply or ceases to apply after a caution has already been given, the person shall be re-cautioned in the appropriate terms. The changed position on drawing inferences and that the previous caution no longer applies shall also be explained to the detainee in ordinary language. See *Note C2*

Notes for guidance

C1   The restriction on drawing inferences from silence does not apply to a person who has not been detained and who therefore cannot be prevented from seeking legal advice if they want to, see paragraphs 10.2 and 3.15.

C2   The following is suggested as a framework to help explain changes in the position on drawing adverse inferences if the restriction on drawing adverse inferences from silence:

(a)   begins to apply:

'The caution you were previously given no longer applies. This is because after that caution:

(i)   you asked to speak to a solicitor but have not yet been allowed an opportunity to speak to a solicitor. See paragraph 1(a); or

(ii)   you have been charged with/informed you may be prosecuted. See paragraph 1(b).

'This means that from now on, adverse inferences cannot be drawn at court and your defence will not be harmed just because you choose to say nothing. Please listen carefully to the caution I am about to give you because it will apply from now on. You will see that it does not say anything about your defence being harmed.'

(b)   ceases to apply before or at the time the person is charged or informed they may be prosecuted, see paragraph 1(a);

'The caution you were previously given no longer applies. This is because after that caution you have been allowed an opportunity to speak to a solicitor. Please listen carefully to the caution I am about to give you because it will apply from now on. It explains how your defence at court may be affected if you choose to say nothing.'

ANNEX D – WRITTEN STATEMENTS UNDER CAUTION

(a)   Written by a person under caution

1.   A person shall always be invited to write down what they want to say.

2.   A person who has not been charged with, or informed they may be prosecuted for, any offence to which the statement they want to write relates, shall:

(a)   unless the statement is made at a time when the restriction on drawing adverse inferences from silence applies, see Annex C, be asked to write out and sign the following before writing what they want to say:

'I make this statement of my own free will. I understand that I do not have to say anything but that it may harm my defence if I do not mention when questioned something which I later rely on in court. This statement may be given in evidence.';

(b)   if the statement is made at a time when the restriction on drawing adverse inferences from silence applies, be asked to write out and sign the following before writing what they want to say;

'I make this statement of my own free will. I understand that I do not have to say anything. This statement may be given in evidence.'

3.   When a person, on the occasion of being charged with or informed they may be prosecuted for any offence, asks to make a statement which relates to any such offence and wants to write it they shall:

(a)   unless the restriction on drawing adverse inferences from silence, see *Annex C*, applied when they were so charged or informed they may be prosecuted, be asked to write out and sign the following before writing what they want to say:

'I make this statement of my own free will. I understand that I do not have to say anything but that it may harm my defence if I do not mention when questioned something which I later rely on in court. This statement may be given in evidence.';

(b)   if the restriction on drawing adverse inferences from silence applied when they were so charged or informed they may be prosecuted, be asked to write out and sign the following before writing what they want to say:

'I make this statement of my own free will. I understand that I do not have to say anything. This statement may be given in evidence.'

4.   When a person, who has already been charged with or informed they may be prosecuted for any offence, asks to make a statement which relates to any such offence and wants to write it they shall be asked to write out and sign the following before writing what they want to say:

'I make this statement of my own free will. I understand that I do not have to say anything. This statement may be given in evidence.';

5.   Any person writing their own statement shall be allowed to do so without any prompting except a police officer or other police staff may indicate to them which matters are material or question any ambiguity in the statement.

(b)   Written by a police officer or other police staff

6.   If a person says they would like someone to write the statement for them, a police officer, or other police staff shall write the statement.

7.   If the person has not been charged with, or informed they may be prosecuted for, any offence to which the statement they want to make relates they shall, before starting, be asked to sign, or make their mark, to the following:

(a)   unless the statement is made at a time when the restriction on drawing adverse inferences from silence applies, see Annex C:

'I, ..., wish to make a statement. I want someone to write down what I say. I understand that I do not have to say anything but that it may harm my defence if I do not mention when questioned something which I later rely on in court. This statement may be given in evidence.';

(b)   if the statement is made at a time when the restriction on drawing adverse inferences from silence applies:

'I, ..., wish to make a statement. I want someone to write down what I say. I understand that I do not have to say anything. This statement may be given in evidence.'

8.   If, on the occasion of being charged with or informed they may be prosecuted for any offence, the person asks to make a statement which relates to any such offence they shall before starting be asked to sign, or make their mark to, the following:

(a)   unless the restriction on drawing adverse inferences from silence applied, see Annex C, when they were so charged or informed they may be prosecuted:

'I, ..., wish to make a statement. I want someone to write down what I say. I understand that I do not have to say anything but that it may harm

my defence if I do not mention when questioned something which I later rely on in court. This statement may be given in evidence.';

(b)   if the restriction on drawing adverse inferences from silence applied when they were so charged or informed they may be prosecuted:

'I, ..., wish to make a statement. I want someone to write down what I say. I understand that I do not have to say anything. This statement may be given in evidence.'

C

9.   If, having already been charged with or informed they may be prosecuted for any offence, a person asks to make a statement which relates to any such offence they shall before starting, be asked to sign, or make their mark to:

'I, ..., wish to make a statement. I want someone to write down what I say. I understand that I do not have to say anything. This statement may be given in evidence.'

10.   The person writing the statement must take down the exact words spoken by the person making it and must not edit or paraphrase it. Any questions that are necessary, e.g. to make it more intelligible, and the answers given must be recorded at the same time on the statement form.

11.   When the writing of a statement is finished the person making it shall be asked to read it and to make any corrections, alterations or additions they want. When they have finished reading they shall be asked to write and sign or make their mark on the following certificate at the end of the statement:

'I have read the above statement, and I have been able to correct, alter or add anything I wish. This statement is true. I have made it of my own free will.'

12.   If the person making the statement cannot read, or refuses to read it, or to write the above mentioned certificate at the end of it or to sign it, the person taking the statement shall read it to them and ask them if they would like to correct, alter or add anything and to put their signature or make their mark at the end. The person taking the statement shall certify on the statement itself what has occurred.

ANNEX E – SUMMARY OF PROVISIONS RELATING TO MENTALLY DISORDERED AND OTHERWISE MENTALLY VULNERABLE PEOPLE

1. If an officer has any suspicion, or is told in good faith, that a person of any age may be mentally disordered or otherwise mentally vulnerable, or mentally incapable of understanding the significance of questions or their replies that person shall be treated as mentally disordered or otherwise mentally vulnerable for the purposes of this Code. See *paragraph 1.4*

2. In the case of a person who is mentally disordered or otherwise mentally vulnerable, 'the appropriate adult' means:

    (a)   a relative, guardian or other person responsible for their care or custody;

    (b)   someone experienced in dealing with mentally disordered or mentally vulnerable people but who is not a police officer or employed by the police;

    (c)   failing these, some other responsible adult aged 18 or over who is not a police officer or employed by the police.

    See *paragraph 1.7(b) and Note 1D*

3. If the custody officer authorises the detention of a person who is mentally vulnerable or appears to be suffering from a mental disorder, the custody officer must as soon as practicable inform the appropriate adult of the grounds for detention and the person's whereabouts, and ask the adult to come to the police station to see them. If the appropriate adult:

    •   is already at the station when information is given as in *paragraphs 3.1* to *3.5* the information must be given in their presence

    •   is not at the station when the provisions of *paragraph 3.1* to *3.5* are complied with these provisions must be complied with again in their presence once they arrive.

    See *paragraphs 3.15* to *3.17*

4. If the appropriate adult, having been informed of the right to legal advice, considers legal advice should be taken, the provisions of *section 6* apply as if the mentally disordered or otherwise mentally vulnerable person had requested access to legal advice. See *paragraph 3.19* and *Note E1.*

5. The custody officer must make sure a person receives appropriate clinical attention as soon as reasonably practicable if the person appears to be suffering from a mental disorder or in urgent cases immediately call the nearest health care professional or an ambulance. It is not intended these provisions delay the transfer of a detainee to a

place of safety under the Mental Health Act 1983, section 136 if that is applicable. If an assessment under that Act is to take place at a police station, the custody officer must consider whether an appropriate health care professional should be called to conduct an initial clinical check on the detainee. See *paragraph 9.5* and *9.6*

6. It is imperative a mentally disordered or otherwise mentally vulnerable person detained under the Mental Health Act 1983, section 136 be assessed as soon as possible. If that assessment is to take place at the police station, an approved social worker and registered medical practitioner shall be called to the station as soon as possible in order to interview and examine the detainee. Once the detainee has been interviewed, examined and suitable arrangements been made for their treatment or care, they can no longer be detained under section 136. A detainee should be immediately discharged from detention if a registered medical practitioner having examined them, concludes they are not mentally disordered within the meaning of the Act. See *paragraph 3.16*

7. If a mentally disordered or otherwise mentally vulnerable person is cautioned in the absence of the appropriate adult, the caution must be repeated in the appropriate adult's presence. See *paragraph 10.12*

8. A mentally disordered or otherwise mentally vulnerable person must not be interviewed or asked to provide or sign a written statement in the absence of the appropriate adult unless the provisions of *paragraphs 11.1* or *11.18* to *11.20* apply. Questioning in these circumstances may not continue in the absence of the appropriate adult once sufficient information to avert the risk has been obtained. A record shall be made of the grounds for any decision to begin an interview in these circumstances. See *paragraphs 11.1, 11.15* and *11.18* to *11.20*

9. If the appropriate adult is present at an interview, they shall be informed they are not expected to act simply as an observer and the purposes of their presence are to:

   • advise the interviewee

   • observe whether or not the interview is being conducted properly and fairly

   • facilitate communication with the interviewee

   See *paragraph 11.17*

10. If the detention of a mentally disordered or otherwise mentally vulnerable person is reviewed by a review officer or a superintendent, the appropriate adult must, if available at the time, be given an opportunity to make representations to the officer about the need for continuing detention. See *paragraph 15.3*

C

11. If the custody officer charges a mentally disordered or otherwise mentally vulnerable person with an offence or takes such other action as is appropriate when there is sufficient evidence for a prosecution this must be done in the presence of the appropriate adult. The written notice embodying any charge must be given to the appropriate adult. See *paragraphs 16.1 to 16.4A*

12. An intimate or strip search of a mentally disordered or otherwise mentally vulnerable person may take place only in the presence of the appropriate adult of the same sex, unless the detainee specifically requests the presence of a particular adult of the opposite sex. A strip search may take place in the absence of an appropriate adult only in cases of urgency when there is a risk of serious harm to the detainee or others. See *Annex A, paragraphs 5 and 11(c)*

13. Particular care must be taken when deciding whether to use any form of approved restraints on a mentally disordered or otherwise mentally vulnerable person in a locked cell. See *paragraph 8.2*

Notes for guidance

E1 *The purpose of the provision at paragraph 3.19 is to protect the rights of a mentally disordered or otherwise mentally vulnerable detained person who does not understand the significance of what is said to them. If the detained person wants to exercise the right to legal advice, the appropriate action should be taken and not delayed until the appropriate adult arrives. A mentally disordered or otherwise mentally vulnerable detained person should always be given an opportunity, when an appropriate adult is called to the police station, to consult privately with a solicitor in the absence of the appropriate adult if they want.*

E2 *Although people who are mentally disordered or otherwise mentally vulnerable are often capable of providing reliable evidence, they may, without knowing or wanting to do so, be particularly prone in certain circumstances to provide information that may be unreliable, misleading or self-incriminating. Special care should always be taken when questioning such a person, and the appropriate adult should be involved if there is any doubt about a person's mental state or capacity. Because of the risk of unreliable evidence, it is important to obtain corroboration of any facts admitted whenever possible.*

E3 *Because of the risks referred to in Note E2, which the presence of the appropriate adult is intended to minimise, officers of superintendent rank or above should exercise their discretion to authorise the commencement of an interview in the appropriate adult's absence only in exceptional cases, if it is necessary to avert an immediate risk of serious harm. See paragraphs 11.1, 11.18 to 11.20*

ANNEX F – COUNTRIES WITH WHICH BILATERAL CONSULAR CONVENTIONS OR AGREEMENTS REQUIRING NOTIFICATION OF THE ARREST AND DETENTION OF THEIR NATIONALS ARE IN FORCE AS AT 1 APRIL 2003

Armenia	Kazakhstan
Austria	Macedonia
Azerbaijan	Mexico
Belarus	Moldova
Belgium	Mongolia
Bosnia-Herzegovina	Norway
Bulgaria	Poland
China*	Romania
Croatia	Russia
Cuba	Slovak Republic
Czech Republic	Slovenia
Denmark	Spain
Egypt	Sweden
France	Tajikistan
Georgia	Turkmenistan
German Federal Republic	Ukraine
Greece	USA
Hungary	Uzbekistan
Italy	Yugoslavia
Japan	

* Police are required to inform Chinese officials of arrest/detention in the Manchester consular district only. This comprises Derbyshire, Durham, Greater Manchester, Lancashire, Merseyside, North South and West Yorkshire, and Tyne and Wear.

ANNEX G – FITNESS TO BE INTERVIEWED

1. This Annex contains general guidance to help police officers and health care professionals assess whether a detainee might be at risk in an interview.

2. A detainee may be at risk in a interview if it is considered that:

    (a) conducting the interview could significantly harm the detainee's physical or mental state;

    (b) anything the detainee says in the interview about their involvement or suspected involvement in the offence about which they are being interviewed **might** be considered unreliable in subsequent court proceedings because of their physical or mental state.

3. In assessing whether the detainee should be interviewed, the following must be considered:

    (a) how the detainee's physical or mental state might affect their ability to understand the nature and purpose of the interview, to comprehend what is being asked and to appreciate the significance of any answers given and make rational decisions about whether they want to say anything;

    (b) the extent to which the detainee's replies may be affected by their physical or mental condition rather than representing a rational and accurate explanation of their involvement in the offence;

    (c) how the nature of the interview, which could include particularly probing questions, might affect the detainee.

4. It is essential health care professionals who are consulted consider the functional ability of the detainee rather than simply relying on a medical diagnosis, e.g. it is possible for a person with severe mental illness to be fit for interview.

5. Health care professionals should advise on the need for an appropriate adult to be present, whether reassessment of the person's fitness for interview may be necessary if the interview lasts beyond a specified time, and whether a further specialist opinion may be required.

6. When health care professionals identify risks they should be asked to quantify the risks. They should inform the custody officer:

    • whether the person's condition:

        – is likely to improve

–　　will require or be amenable to treatment; and

• 　　indicate how long it may take for such improvement to take effect

7. The role of the health care professional is to consider the risks and advise the custody officer of the outcome of that consideration. The health care professional's determination and any advice or recommendations should be made in writing and form part of the custody record.

8. Once the health care professional has provided that information, it is a matter for the custody officer to decide whether or not to allow the interview to go ahead and if the interview is to proceed, to determine what safeguards are needed. Nothing prevents safeguards being provided in addition to those required under the Code. An example might be to have an appropriate health care professional present during the interview, in addition to an appropriate adult, in order constantly to monitor the person's condition and how it is being affected by the interview.

ANNEX H – DETAINED PERSON: OBSERVATION LIST

1.   If any detainee fails to meet any of the following criteria, an appropriate health care professional or an ambulance must be called.

2.   When assessing the level of rousability, consider:

Rousability – can they be woken?

* go into the cell

* call their name

* shake gently

Response to questions – can they give appropriate answers to questions such as:

* What's your name?

* Where do you live?

* Where do you think you are?

Response to commands – can they respond appropriately to commands such as:

* Open your eyes!

* Lift one arm, now the other arm!

3.   Remember to take into account the possibility or presence of other illnesses, injury, or mental condition, a person who is drowsy and smells of alcohol may also have the following:

* Diabetes

* Epilepsy

* Head injury

* Drug intoxication or overdose

* Stroke

ANNEX I – Not Used

ANNEX J – Not Used

ANNEX K – X-RAYS AND ULTRASOUND SCANS

(a) Action

1. PACE, section 55A allows a person who has been arrested and is in police detention to have an X-ray taken of them or an ultrasound scan to be carried out on them (or both) if:

    (a) authorised by an officer of inspector rank or above who has reasonable grounds for believing that the detainee:

        (i) may have swallowed a Class A drug; and

        (ii) was in possession of that Class A drug with the intention of supplying it to another or to export; and

    (b) the detainee's appropriate consent has been given in writing.

2. Before an x-ray is taken or an ultrasound scan carried out, a police officer, designated detention officer or staff custody officer must tell the detainee:-

    (a) that the authority has been given; and

    (b) the grounds for giving the authorisation.

3. Before a detainee is asked to give appropriate consent to an x-ray or an ultrasound scan, they must be warned that if they refuse without good cause their refusal may harm their case if it comes to trial, see *Notes K1* and *K2*. This warning may be given by a police officer or member of police staff. A detainee who is not legally represented must be reminded of their entitlement to have free legal advice, see Code C, *paragraph 6.5*, and the reminder noted in the custody record.

4. An x-ray may be taken, or an ultrasound scan may be carried out, only by a registered medical practitioner or registered nurse, and only at a hospital, surgery or other medical premises.

(b)   Documentation

5.   The following shall be recorded as soon as practicable in the detainee's custody record:

(a)   the authorisation to take the x-ray or carry out the ultrasound scan (or both);

(b)   the grounds for giving the authorisation;

(c)   the giving of the warning required by *paragraph 3*; and

(d)   the fact that the appropriate consent was given or (as the case may be) refused, and if refused, the reason given for the refusal (if any); and

(e)   if an x-ray is taken or an ultrasound scan carried out:

- where it was taken or carried out

- who took it or carried it out

- who was present

- the result

6   Paragraphs 1.4 – 1.7 of this Code apply and an appropriate adult should be present when consent is sought to any procedure under this Annex.

Notes for guidance

K1   *If authority is given for an x-ray to be taken or an ultrasound scan to be carried out (or both), consideration should be given to asking a registered medical practitioner or registered nurse to explain to the detainee what is involved and to allay any concerns the detainee might have about the effect which taking an x-ray or carrying out an ultrasound scan might have on them. If appropriate consent is not given, evidence of the explanation may, if the case comes to trial, be relevant to determining whether the detainee had a good cause for refusing.*

K2   *In warning a detainee who is asked to consent to an X-ray being taken or an ultrasound scan being carried out (or both), as in paragraph 3, the following form of words may be used:*

"You do not have to allow an x-ray of you to be taken or an ultrasound scan to be carried out on you, but I must warn you that if you refuse without good cause, your refusal may harm your case if it comes to trial."

POLICE & CRIMINAL EVIDENCE ACT 1984 (PACE)

CODE H

CODE OF PRACTICE IN CONNECTION WITH THE DETENTION, TREATMENT AND QUESTIONING BY POLICE OFFICERS OF PERSONS UNDER SECTION 41 OF, AND SCHEDULE 8 TO, THE TERRORISM ACT 2000

Commencement – Transitional Arrangements

This Code applies to people in police detention following their arrest under section 41 of the Terrorism Act 2000, after midnight (on 24 July 2006), notwithstanding that they may have been arrested before that time.

1   General

1.1   This Code of Practice applies to, and only to, persons arrested under section 41 of the Terrorism Act 2000 (TACT) and detained in police custody under those provisions and Schedule 8 of the Act. References to detention under this provision that were previously included in PACE Code C – Code for the Detention, Treatment, and Questioning of Persons by Police Officers, no longer apply.

1.2   The Code ceases to apply at any point that a detainee is:

(a)   charged with an offence

(b)   released without charge,or

(c)   transferred to a prison see *section 14.5*

1.3   References to an offence in this Code include being concerned in the commission, preparation or instigation of acts of terrorism.

1.4   This Code's provisions do not apply to detention of individuals under any other terrorism legislation. This Code does not apply to people:

(i)   detained under section 5(1) of the Prevention of Terrorism Act 2005.

(ii)   detained for examination under TACT Schedule 7 and to whom the Code of Practice issued under that Act, Schedule 14, paragraph 6 applies;

(iii)   detained for searches under stop and search powers.

The provisions for the detention, treatment and questioning by police officers of persons other than those in police detention following arrest under section 41 of TACT, are set out in Code C issued under section 66(1) of the Police & Criminal Evidence Act (PACE)1984 (PACE Code C).

1.5   All persons in custody must be dealt with expeditiously, and released as soon as the need for detention no longer applies.

1.6   There is no provision for bail under TACT prior to charge.

1.7   An officer must perform the assigned duties in this Code as soon as practicable. An officer will not be in breach of this Code if delay is justifiable and reasonable steps are taken to prevent unnecessary delay. The custody record shall show when a delay has occurred and the reason. See *Note 1H*

1.8   This Code of Practice must be readily available at all police stations for consultation by:

• police officers

- police staff

- detained persons

- members of the public.

1.9 The provisions of this Code:

- include the *Annexes*

- do not include the *Notes for Guidance*.

1.10 If an officer has any suspicion, or is told in good faith, that a person of any age may be mentally disordered or otherwise mentally vulnerable, in the absence of clear evidence to dispel that suspicion, the person shall be treated as such for the purposes of this Code. See *Note 1G*

1.11 For the purposes of this Code, a juvenile is any person under the age of 17. If anyone appears to be under 17, and there is no clear evidence that they are 17 or over, they shall be treated as a juvenile for the purposes of this Code.

1.12 If a person appears to be blind, seriously visually impaired, deaf, unable to read or speak or has difficulty orally because of a speech impediment, they shall be treated as such for the purposes of this Code in the absence of clear evidence to the contrary.

1.13 'The appropriate adult' means, in the case of a:

(a) juvenile:

    (i) the parent, guardian or, if the juvenile is in local authority or voluntary organisation care, or is otherwise being looked after under the Children Act 1989, a person representing that authority or organisation;

    (ii) a social worker of a local authority social services department;

    (iii) failing these, some other responsible adult aged 18 or over who is not a police officer or employed by the police.

(b) person who is mentally disordered or mentally vulnerable: See *Note 1D*

    (i) a relative, guardian or other person responsible for their care or custody;

    (ii) someone experienced in dealing with mentally disordered or mentally vulnerable people but who is not a police officer or employed by the police;

    (iii) failing these, some other responsible adult aged 18 or over who is not a police officer or employed by the police.

H

1.14 If this Code requires a person be given certain information, they do not have to be given it if at the time they are incapable of understanding what is said, are violent or may become violent or in urgent need of medical attention, but they must be given it as soon as practicable.

1.15 References to a custody officer include any:-

- police officer; or

- designated staff custody officer acting in the exercise or performance of the powers and duties conferred or imposed on them by their designation,

performing the functions of a custody officer. See *Note 1J*.

1.16 When this Code requires the prior authority or agreement of an officer of at least inspector or superintendent rank, that authority may be given by a sergeant or chief inspector authorised by section 107 of PACE to perform the functions of the higher rank under TACT.

1.17 In this Code:

(a) 'designated person' means a person other than a police officer, designated under the Police Reform Act 2002, Part 4 who has specified powers and duties of police officers conferred or imposed on them;

(b) reference to a police officer includes a designated person acting in the exercise or performance of the powers and duties conferred or imposed on them by their designation.

1.18 Designated persons are entitled to use reasonable force as follows:-

(a) when exercising a power conferred on them which allows a police officer exercising that power to use reasonable force, a designated person has the same entitlement to use force; and

(b) at other times when carrying out duties conferred or imposed on them that also entitle them to use reasonable force, for example:

- when at a police station carrying out the duty to keep detainees for whom they are responsible under control and to assist any other police officer or designated person to keep any detainee under control and to prevent their escape.

- when securing, or assisting any other police officer or designated person in securing, the detention of a person at a police station.

- when escorting, or assisting any other police officer or designated person in escorting, a detainee within a police station.

- for the purpose of saving life or limb; or

- preventing serious damage to property.

1.19 Nothing in this Code prevents the custody officer, or other officer given custody of the detainee, from allowing police staff who are not designated persons to carry out individual procedures or tasks at the police station if the law allows. However, the officer remains responsible for making sure the procedures and tasks are carried out correctly in accordance with the Codes of Practice. Any such person must be:

(a) a person employed by a police authority maintaining a police force and under the control and direction of the Chief Officer of that force;

(b) employed by a person with whom a police authority has a contract for the provision of services relating to persons arrested or otherwise in custody.

1.20 Designated persons and other police staff must have regard to any relevant provisions of this Code.

1.21 References to pocket books include any official report book issued to police officers or other police staff.

Notes for guidance

1A *Although certain sections of this Code apply specifically to people in custody at police stations, those there voluntarily to assist with an investigation should be treated with no less consideration, e.g. offered refreshments at appropriate times, and enjoy an absolute right to obtain legal advice or communicate with anyone outside the police station.*

1B *A person, including a parent or guardian, should not be an appropriate adult if they:*

- *are*

  - *suspected of involvement in the offence or involvement in the commission, preparation or instigation of acts of terrorism*

  - *the victim*

  - *a witness*

  - *involved in the investigation*

- *received admissions prior to attending to act as the appropriate adult.*

H

Note: If a juvenile's parent is estranged from the juvenile, they should not be asked to act as the appropriate adult if the juvenile expressly and specifically objects to their presence.

1C *If a juvenile admits an offence to, or in the presence of, a social worker or member of a youth offending team other than during the time that person is acting as the juvenile's appropriate adult, another appropriate adult should be appointed in the interest of fairness.*

1D *In the case of people who are mentally disordered or otherwise mentally vulnerable, it may be more satisfactory if the appropriate adult is someone experienced or trained in their care rather than a relative lacking such qualifications. But if the detainee prefers a relative to a better qualified stranger or objects to a particular person their wishes should, if practicable, be respected.*

1E *A detainee should always be given an opportunity, when an appropriate adult is called to the police station, to consult privately with a solicitor in the appropriate adult's absence if they want. An appropriate adult is not subject to legal privilege.*

1F *A solicitor or independent custody visitor (formerly a lay visitor) present at the police station in that capacity may not be the appropriate adult.*

1G *'Mentally vulnerable' applies to any detainee who, because of their mental state or capacity, may not understand the significance of what is said, of questions or of their replies. 'Mental disorder' is defined in the Mental Health Act 1983, section 1(2) as 'mental illness, arrested or incomplete development of mind, psychopathic disorder and any other disorder or disability of mind'. When the custody officer has any doubt about the mental state or capacity of a detainee, that detainee should be treated as mentally vulnerable and an appropriate adult called.*

1H *Paragraph 1.7 is intended to cover delays which may occur in processing detainees e.g if:*

- *a large number of suspects are brought into the station simultaneously to be placed in custody;*

- *interview rooms are all being used;*

- *there are difficulties contacting an appropriate adult, solicitor or interpreter.*

1I *The custody officer must remind the appropriate adult and detainee about the right to legal advice and record any reasons for waiving it in accordance with section 6.*

1J   *The designation of police staff custody officers applies only in police areas where an order commencing the provisions of the Police Reform Act 2002, section 38 and Schedule 4A, for designating police staff custody officers is in effect.*

1K   *This Code does not affect the principle that all citizens have a duty to help police officers to prevent crime and discover offenders. This is a civic rather than a legal duty; but when a police officer is trying to discover whether, or by whom, an offence has been committed he is entitled to question any person from whom he thinks useful information can be obtained, subject to the restrictions imposed by this Code. A person's declaration that he is unwilling to reply does not alter this entitlement.*

1L   *If a person is moved from a police station to receive medical treatment, or for any other reason, the period of detention is still calculated from the time of arrest under section 41 of TACT (or, if a person was being detained under TACT Schedule 7 when arrested, from the time at which the examination under Schedule 7 began).*

1M   Under Paragraph 1 of Schedule 8 to TACT, all police stations are designated for detention of persons arrested under section 41 of TACT. Paragraph 4 of Schedule 8 requires that the constable who arrests a person under section 41 takes him as soon as practicable to the police station which he considers is "most appropriate".

2   Custody records

2.1   When a person is brought to a police station:

- under TACT section 41 arrest, or

- is arrested under TACT section 41 at the police station having attended there voluntarily,

they should be brought before the custody officer as soon as practicable after their arrival at the station or, if appropriate, following arrest after attending the police station voluntarily *see Note 3H*. A person is deemed to be "at a police station" for these purposes if they are within the boundary of any building or enclosed yard which forms part of that police station.

2.2   A separate custody record must be opened as soon as practicable for each person brought to a police station under arrest or arrested at the station having gone there voluntarily. All information recorded under this Code must be recorded as soon as practicable in the custody record unless otherwise specified. Any audio or video recording made in the custody area is not part of the custody record.

2.3   If any action requires the authority of an officer of a specified rank, this must be noted in the custody record, subject to paragraph 2.8.

H

2.4 The custody officer is responsible for the custody record's accuracy and completeness and for making sure the record or copy of the record accompanies a detainee if they are transferred to another police station. The record shall show the:

- time and reason for transfer;

- time a person is released from detention.

2.5 A solicitor or appropriate adult must be permitted to consult a detainee's custody record as soon as practicable after their arrival at the station and at any other time whilst the person is detained. Arrangements for this access must be agreed with the custody officer and may not unreasonably interfere with the custody officer's duties or the justifiable needs of the investigation.

2.6 When a detainee leaves police detention or is taken before a court they, their legal representative or appropriate adult shall be given, on request, a copy of the custody record as soon as practicable. This entitlement lasts for 12 months after release.

2.7 The detainee, appropriate adult or legal representative shall be permitted to inspect the original custody record once the detained person is no longer held under the provisions of TACT section 41 and Schedule 8, provided they give reasonable notice of their request. Any such inspection shall be noted in the custody record.

2.8 All entries in custody records must be timed and identified by the maker. Nothing in this Code requires the identity of officers or other police staff to be recorded or disclosed in the case of enquiries linked to the investigation of terrorism. In these cases, they shall use their warrant or other identification numbers and the name of their police station *see Note 2A*. If records are entered on computer these shall also be timed and contain the operator's identification.

2.9 The fact and time of any detainee's refusal to sign a custody record, when asked in accordance with this Code, must be recorded.

Note for guidance

2A *The purpose of paragraph 2.8 is to protect those involved in terrorist investigations or arrests of terrorist suspects from the possibility that those arrested, their associates or other individuals or groups may threaten or cause harm to those involved.*

3   Initial action

(a)   Detained persons – normal procedure

3.1   When a person is brought to a police station under arrest or arrested at the station having gone there voluntarily, the custody officer must make sure the person is told clearly about the following continuing rights which may be exercised at any stage during the period in custody:

(i)   the right to have someone informed of their arrest as in *section 5*;

(ii)   the right to consult privately with a solicitor and that free independent legal advice is available;

(iii)   the right to consult this Code of Practice. See *Note 3D*

3.2   The detainee must also be given:

- a written notice setting out:

    –   the above three rights;

    –   the arrangements for obtaining legal advice;

    –   the right to a copy of the custody record as in *paragraph 2.6;*

    –   the caution in the terms prescribed in *section 10.*

- an additional written notice briefly setting out their entitlements while in custody, see *Notes 3A* and *3B.*

Note: The detainee shall be asked to sign the custody record to acknowledge receipt of these notices. Any refusal must be recorded on the custody record.

3.3   A citizen of an independent Commonwealth country or a national of a foreign country, including the Republic of Ireland, must be informed as soon as practicable about their rights of communication with their High Commission, Embassy or Consulate. See *section 7*

3.4   The custody officer shall:

- record that the person was arrested under section 41 of TACT and the reason(s) for the arrest on the custody record. See *paragraph 10.2 and Note for Guidance 3G.*

- note on the custody record any comment the detainee makes in relation to the arresting officer's account but shall not invite comment. If the arresting officer is not physically present when the detainee is brought to a police station, the

H

arresting officer's account must be made available to the custody officer remotely or by a third party on the arresting officer's behalf;

- note any comment the detainee makes in respect of the decision to detain them but shall not invite comment;

- not put specific questions to the detainee regarding their involvement in any offence, nor in respect of any comments they may make in response to the arresting officer's account or the decision to place them in detention *See paragraphs 14.1* and *14.2* and *Notes for Guidance 3H, 14A* and *14B*. Such an exchange is likely to constitute an interview as in *paragraph 11.1* and require the associated safeguards in *section 11*.

See *paragraph 5.9 of the Code of Practice issued under TACT Schedule 8 Paragraph 3* in respect of unsolicited comments.

If the first review of detention is carried out at this time, see paragraphs 14.1 and 14.2, and Part II of Schedule 8 to the Terrorism Act 2000 in respect of action by the review officer.

3.5   The custody officer shall:

(a)   ask the detainee, whether at this time, they:

(vii)   would like legal advice, see *section 6*;

(viii)   want someone informed of their detention, see *section 5*;

(b)   ask the detainee to sign the custody record to confirm their decisions in respect of (*a*);

(c)   determine whether the detainee:

(i)   is, or might be, in need of medical treatment or attention, see *section 9*;

(ii)   requires:

- an appropriate adult;

- help to check documentation;

- an interpreter;

(d)   record the decision in respect of (*c*).

3.6   When determining these needs the custody officer is responsible for initiating an assessment to consider whether the detainee is likely to present specific risks to custody staff, any individual who may have contact with detainee (e.g. legal advisers, medical staff), or themselves. Such assessments should always include a check on the Police National Computer, to be carried out as soon as practicable, to identify any risks highlighted in relation to the detainee. Although such assessments are primarily the custody officer's responsibility, it will be necessary to obtain information from other sources, especially the investigation team *See Note 3E*, the arresting officer or an appropriate health care professional, see *paragraph 9.15*. Reasons for delaying the initiation or completion of the assessment must be recorded.

H

3.7 Chief Officers should ensure that arrangements for proper and effective risk assessments required by *paragraph 3.6* are implemented in respect of all detainees at police stations in their area.

3.8 Risk assessments must follow a structured process which clearly defines the categories of risk to be considered and the results must be incorporated in the detainee's custody record. The custody officer is responsible for making sure those responsible for the detainee's custody are appropriately briefed about the risks. The content of any risk assessment and any analysis of the level of risk relating to the person's detention is not required to be shown or provided to the detainee or any person acting on behalf of the detainee. If no specific risks are identified by the assessment, that should be noted in the custody record. See *Note 3F* and *paragraph 9.15*

3.9 Custody officers are responsible for implementing the response to any specific risk assessment, which should include for example:

- reducing opportunities for self harm;

- calling a health care professional;

- increasing levels of monitoring or observation;

- reducing the risk to those who come into contact with the detainee .

See Note for Guidance 3F

3.10 Risk assessment is an ongoing process and assessments must always be subject to review if circumstances change.

3.11 If video cameras are installed in the custody area, notices shall be prominently displayed showing cameras are in use. Any request to have video cameras switched off shall be refused.

3.12 A constable, prison officer or other person authorised by the Secretary of State may take any steps which are reasonably necessary for

(a) photographing the detained person

    (b)   measuring him, or

    (c)   identifying him.

3.13   Paragraph 3.12 concerns the power in TACT Schedule 8 Paragraph 2. The power in TACT Schedule 8 Paragraph 2 does not cover the taking of fingerprints, intimate samples or non-intimate samples, which is covered in TACT Schedule 8 paragraphs 10-15.

H

(b)   Detained persons – special groups

3.14   If the detainee appears deaf or there is doubt about their hearing or speaking ability or ability to understand English, and the custody officer cannot establish effective communication, the custody officer must, as soon as practicable, call an interpreter for assistance in the action under *paragraphs 3.1–3.5*. See *section 13*

3.15   If the detainee is a juvenile, the custody officer must, if it is practicable, ascertain the identity of a person responsible for their welfare. That person:

- may be:

    – the parent or guardian;

    – if the juvenile is in local authority or voluntary organisation care, or is otherwise being looked after under the Children Act 1989, a person appointed by that authority or organisation to have responsibility for the juvenile's welfare;

    – any other person who has, for the time being, assumed responsibility for the juvenile's welfare.

- must be informed as soon as practicable that the juvenile has been arrested, why they have been arrested and where they are detained. This right is in addition to the juvenile's right in *section 5* not to be held incommunicado. See *Note 3C*

3.16   If a juvenile is known to be subject to a court order under which a person or organisation is given any degree of statutory responsibility to supervise or otherwise monitor them, reasonable steps must also be taken to notify that person or organisation (the 'responsible officer'). The responsible officer will normally be a member of a Youth Offending Team, except for a curfew order which involves electronic monitoring when the contractor providing the monitoring will normally be the responsible officer.

3.17 If the detainee is a juvenile, mentally disordered or otherwise mentally vulnerable, the custody officer must, as soon as practicable:

- inform the appropriate adult, who in the case of a juvenile may or may not be a person responsible for their welfare, as in *paragraph 3.15,* of:

    - the grounds for their detention;

    - their whereabouts.

- ask the adult to come to the police station to see the detainee.

3.18 If the appropriate adult is:

- already at the police station, the provisions of *paragraphs 3.1* to *3.5* must be complied with in the appropriate adult's presence;

- not at the station when these provisions are complied with, they must be complied with again in the presence of the appropriate adult when they arrive.

3.19 The detainee shall be advised that:

- the duties of the appropriate adult include giving advice and assistance;

- they can consult privately with the appropriate adult at any time.

3.20 If the detainee, or appropriate adult on the detainee's behalf, asks for a solicitor to be called to give legal advice, the provisions of *section 6* apply.

3.21 If the detainee is blind, seriously visually impaired or unable to read, the custody officer shall make sure their solicitor, relative, appropriate adult or some other person likely to take an interest in them and not involved in the investigation is available to help check any documentation. When this Code requires written consent or signing the person assisting may be asked to sign instead, if the detainee prefers. This paragraph does not require an appropriate adult to be called solely to assist in checking and signing documentation for a person who is not a juvenile, or mentally disordered or otherwise mentally vulnerable (see *paragraph 3.17*).

(c) **Documentation**

3.22 The grounds for a person's detention shall be recorded, in the person's presence if practicable.

3.23 Action taken under *paragraphs 3.14* to *3.22* shall be recorded.

H

Notes for guidance

3A   The notice of entitlements should:

- list the entitlements in this Code, including:

  - visits and contact with outside parties where practicable, including special provisions for Commonwealth citizens and foreign nationals;

  - reasonable standards of physical comfort;

  - adequate food and drink;

  - access to toilets and washing facilities, clothing, medical attention, and exercise when practicable.

- mention the:

  - provisions relating to the conduct of interviews;

  - circumstances in which an appropriate adult should be available to assist the detainee and their statutory rights to make representation whenever the period of their detention is reviewed.

3B   In addition to notices in English, translations should be available in Welsh, the main minority ethnic languages and the principal European languages whenever they are likely to be helpful. Audio versions of the notice should also be made available.

3C   If the juvenile is in local authority or voluntary organisation care but living with their parents or other adults responsible for their welfare, although there is no legal obligation to inform them, they should normally be contacted, as well as the authority or organisation unless suspected of involvement in the offence concerned. Even if the juvenile is not living with their parents, consideration should be given to informing them.

3D   The right to consult this or other relevant Codes of Practice does not entitle the person concerned to delay unreasonably any necessary investigative or administrative action whilst they do so. Examples of action which need not be delayed unreasonably include:

- searching detainees at the police station;

- taking fingerprints or non-intimate samples without consent for evidential purposes.

3E   The investigation team will include any officer involved in questioning a suspect, gathering or analysing evidence in relation to the offences of which the detainee is suspected of

96

having committed. Should a custody officer require information from the investigation team, the first point of contact should be the officer in charge of the investigation.

3F *Home Office Circular 32/2000 provides more detailed guidance on risk assessments and identifies key risk areas which should always be considered. This should be read with the Guidance on Safer Detention & Handling of Persons in Police Custody issued by the National Centre for Policing Excellence in conjunction with the Home Office and Association of Chief Police Officers.*

3G *Arrests under TACT section 41 can only be made where an officer has reasonable grounds to suspect that the individual concerned is a "terrorist". This differs from the PACE power of arrest in that it need not be linked to a specific offence. There may also be circumstances where an arrest under TACT is made on the grounds of sensitive information which can not be disclosed. In such circumstances, the grounds for arrest may be given in terms of the interpretation of a "terrorist" set out in TACT sections 40(1)(a) or 40(1)(b).*

3H *For the purpose of arrests under TACT section 41, the review officer is responsible for authorising detention (see Paragraphs 14.1 and 14.2, and Notes for Guidance 14A and 14B). The review officer's role is explained in TACT Schedule 8 Part II. A person may be detained after arrest pending the first review, which must take place as soon as practicable after the person's arrest.*

4   Detainee's property

(a)   Action

4.1   The custody officer is responsible for:

(a)   ascertaining what property a detainee:

   (i)   has with them when they come to the police station, either on first arrival at the police station or any subsequent arrivals at a police station in connection with that detention.

   (ii)   might have acquired for an unlawful or harmful purpose while in custody;

(b)   the safekeeping of any property taken from a detainee which remains at the police station.

The custody officer may search the detainee or authorise their being searched to the extent they consider necessary, provided a search of intimate parts of the body or involving the removal of more than outer clothing is only made as in *Annex A*. A search may only be carried out by an officer of the same sex as the detainee. See *Note 4A*

4.2 Detainees may retain clothing and personal effects at their own risk unless the custody officer considers they may use them to cause harm to themselves or others, interfere with evidence, damage property, effect an escape or they are needed as evidence. In this event the custody officer may withhold such articles as they consider necessary and must tell the detainee why.

4.3 Personal effects are those items a detainee may lawfully need, use or refer to while in detention but do not include cash and other items of value.

(b) Documentation

4.4 It is a matter for the custody officer to determine whether a record should be made of the property a detained person has with him or had taken from him on arrest (see *Note for Guidance 4D*). Any record made is not required to be kept as part of the custody record but the custody record should be noted as to where such a record exists. Whenever a record is made the detainee shall be allowed to check and sign the record of property as correct. Any refusal to sign shall be recorded.

4.5 If a detainee is not allowed to keep any article of clothing or personal effects, the reason must be recorded.

Notes for guidance

4A *PACE, Section 54(1) and paragraph 4.1 require a detainee to be searched when it is clear the custody officer will have continuing duties in relation to that detainee or when that detainee's behaviour or offence makes an inventory appropriate. They do not require every detainee to be searched, e.g. if it is clear a person will only be detained for a short period and is not to be placed in a cell, the custody officer may decide not to search them. In such a case the custody record will be endorsed 'not searched', paragraph 4.4 will not apply, and the detainee will be invited to sign the entry. If the detainee refuses, the custody officer will be obliged to ascertain what property they have in accordance with paragraph 4.1.*

4B *Paragraph 4.4 does not require the custody officer to record on the custody record property in the detainee's possession on arrest if, by virtue of its nature, quantity or size, it is not practicable to remove it to the police station.*

4C *Paragraph 4.4 does not require items of clothing worn by the person be recorded unless withheld by the custody officer as in paragraph 4.2.*

4D *Section 43(2) of TACT allows a constable to search a person who has been arrested under section 41 to discover whether he has anything in his possession that may constitute evidence that he is a terrorist.*

5   Right not to be held incommunicado

(a)   Action

5.1   Any person arrested and held in custody at a police station or other premises may, on request, have one named person who is a friend, relative or a person known to them who is likely to take an interest in their welfare informed at public expense of their whereabouts as soon as practicable. If the person cannot be contacted the detainee may choose up to two alternatives. If they cannot be contacted, the person in charge of detention or the investigation has discretion to allow further attempts until the information has been conveyed. See *Notes 5D* and *5E*

5.2   The exercise of the above right in respect of each person nominated may be delayed only in accordance with *Annex B*.

5.3   The above right may be exercised each time a detainee is taken to another police station or returned to a police station having been previously transferred to prison. This Code does not afford such a right to a person on transfer to a prison, where a detainee's rights will be governed by Prison Rules *see paragraph 14.8.*

5.4   If the detainee agrees, they may receive visits from friends, family or others likely to take an interest in their welfare, at the custody officer's discretion. Custody Officers should liaise closely with the investigation team (see *Note 3E)* to allow risk assessments to be made where particular visitors have been requested by the detainee or identified themselves to police. In circumstances where the nature of the investigation means that such requests can not be met, consideration should be given, in conjunction with a representative of the relevant scheme, to increasing the frequency of visits from independent visitor schemes. See *Notes 5B* and *5C.*

5.5   If a friend, relative or person with an interest in the detainee's welfare enquires about their whereabouts, this information shall be given if the suspect agrees and *Annex B* does not apply. See *Note 5E*

5.6   The detainee shall be given writing materials, on request, and allowed to telephone one person for a reasonable time, see *Notes 5A* and *5F.* Either or both these privileges may be denied or delayed if an officer of inspector rank or above considers sending a letter or making a telephone call may result in any of the consequences in *Annex B paragraphs 1* and *2*, particularly in relation to the making of a telephone call in a language which an officer listening to the call (see paragraph 5.7) does not understand. See *note 5G.*

Nothing in this paragraph permits the restriction or denial of the rights in *paragraphs 5.1* and *6.1.*

H

5.7   Before any letter or message is sent, or telephone call made, the detainee shall be informed that what they say in any letter, call or message (other than in a communication to a solicitor) may be read or listened to and may be given in evidence. A telephone call may be terminated if it is being abused *see Note 5G*. The costs can be at public expense at the custody officer's discretion.

5.8   Any delay or denial of the rights in this section should be proportionate and should last no longer than necessary.

(b)   Documentation

5.9   A record must be kept of any:

(a)   request made under this section and the action taken;

(b)   letters, messages or telephone calls made or received or visit received;

(c)   refusal by the detainee to have information about them given to an outside enquirer, or any refusal to see a visitor. The detainee must be asked to countersign the record accordingly and any refusal recorded.

Notes for guidance

5A   A person may request an interpreter to interpret a telephone call or translate a letter.

5B   At the custody officer's discretion (and subject to the detainee's consent), visits from friends, family or others likely to take an interest in the detainee's welfare, should be allowed when possible, subject to sufficient personnel being available to supervise a visit and any possible hindrance to the investigation. Custody Officers should bear in mind the exceptional nature of prolonged TACT detention and consider the potential benefits that visits may bring to the health and welfare of detainees who are held for extended periods.

5C   Official visitors should be given access following consultation with the officer who has overall responsibility for the investigation provided the detainee consents, and they do not compromise safety or security or unduly delay or interfere with the progress of an investigation. Official visitors should still be required to provide appropriate identification and subject to any screening process in place at the place of detention. Official visitors may include:

•   *An accredited faith representative*

•   *Members of either House of Parliament*

•   *Public officials needing to interview the prisoner in the course of their duties*

- *Other persons visiting with the approval of the officer who has overall responsibility for the investigation*

- *Consular officials visiting a detainee who is a national of the country they represent subject to Annex F.*

Visits from appropriate members of the Independent Custody Visitors Scheme should be dealt with in accordance with the separate Code of Practice on Independent Custody Visiting.

5D   *If the detainee does not know anyone to contact for advice or support or cannot contact a friend or relative, the custody officer should bear in mind any local voluntary bodies or other organisations that might be able to help. Paragraph 6.1 applies if legal advice is required.*

5E   *In some circumstances it may not be appropriate to use the telephone to disclose information under paragraphs 5.1 and 5.5.*

5F   *The telephone call at paragraph 5.6 is in addition to any communication under paragraphs 5.1 and 6.1. Further calls may be made at the custody officer's discretion.*

5G   *The nature of terrorism investigations means that officers should have particular regard to the possibility of suspects attempting to pass information which may be detrimental to public safety, or to an investigation.*

6   Right to legal advice

(a)   Action

6.1   Unless *Annex B* applies, all detainees must be informed that they may at any time consult and communicate privately with a solicitor, whether in person, in writing or by telephone, and that free independent legal advice is available from the duty solicitor. Where an appropriate adult is in attendance, they must also be informed of this right. See *paragraph 3.1, Note 1I, Note 6B* and *Note 6I*

6.2   A poster advertising the right to legal advice must be prominently displayed in the charging area of every police station. See *Note 6G*

6.3   No police officer should, at any time, do or say anything with the intention of dissuading a detainee from obtaining legal advice.

6.4   The exercise of the right of access to legal advice may be delayed exceptionally only as in *Annex B*. Whenever legal advice is requested, and unless *Annex B* applies, the custody officer must act without delay to secure the provision of such advice. If, on being informed or reminded of this right, the detainee declines to speak to a solicitor in person,

H

the officer should point out that the right includes the right to speak with a solicitor on the telephone (see *paragraph 5.6)*. If the detainee continues to waive this right the officer should ask them why and any reasons should be recorded on the custody record or the interview record as appropriate. Reminders of the right to legal advice must be given as in *paragraphs 3.5, 11.3,* and the PACE Code D on the Identification of Persons by Police Officers (PACE Code D), *paragraphs 3.19(ii)* and *6.2*. Once it is clear a detainee does not want to speak to a solicitor in person or by telephone they should cease to be asked their reasons. See *Note 6J*.

6.5   An officer of the rank of Commander or Assistant Chief Constable may give a direction under TACT Schedule 8 paragraph 9 that a detainee may only consult a solicitor within the sight and hearing of a qualified officer. Such a direction may only be given if the officer has reasonable grounds to believe that if it were not, it may result in one of the consequences set out in TACT Schedule 8 paragraphs 8(4) or 8(5)(c). See *Annex B paragraph 3* and *Note 6I*. A "qualified officer" means a police officer who:

(a)   is at least the rank of inspector;

(b)   is of the uniformed branch of the force of which the officer giving the direction is a member, and

(c)   in the opinion of the officer giving the direction, has no connection with the detained person's case

Officers considering the use of this power should first refer to Home Office Circular 40/2003.

6.6   In the case of a juvenile, an appropriate adult should consider whether legal advice from a solicitor is required. If the juvenile indicates that they do not want legal advice, the appropriate adult has the right to ask for a solicitor to attend if this would be in the best interests of the person. However, the detained person cannot be forced to see the solicitor if he is adamant that he does not wish to do so.

6.7   A detainee who wants legal advice may not be interviewed or continue to be interviewed until they have received such advice unless:

(a)   *Annex B* applies, when the restriction on drawing adverse inferences from silence in *Annex C* will apply because the detainee is not allowed an opportunity to consult a solicitor; or

(b)   an officer of superintendent rank or above has reasonable grounds for believing that:

   (i)   the consequent delay might:

   • lead to interference with, or harm to, evidence connected with an offence;

   • lead to interference with, or physical harm to, other people;

   • lead to serious loss of, or damage to, property;

   • lead to alerting other people suspected of having committed an offence but not yet arrested for it;

   • hinder the recovery of property obtained in consequence of the commission of an offence.

   (ii)   when a solicitor, including a duty solicitor, has been contacted and has agreed to attend, awaiting their arrival would cause unreasonable delay to the process of investigation.

Note: In these cases the restriction on drawing adverse inferences from silence in *Annex C* will apply because the detainee is not allowed an opportunity to consult a solicitor.

(c)   the solicitor the detainee has nominated or selected from a list:

   (i)   cannot be contacted;

   (ii)   has previously indicated they do not wish to be contacted; or

   (iii)   having been contacted, has declined to attend; and

the detainee has been advised of the Duty Solicitor Scheme but has declined to ask for the duty solicitor.

In these circumstances the interview may be started or continued without further delay provided an officer of inspector rank or above has agreed to the interview proceeding.

Note: The restriction on drawing adverse inferences from silence in *Annex C* will not apply because the detainee is allowed an opportunity to consult the duty solicitor;

H

(d)   the detainee changes their mind, about wanting legal advice.

In these circumstances the interview may be started or continued without delay provided that:

(i)   the detainee agrees to do so , in writing or on the interview record made in accordance with the Code of Practice issued under TACT Schedule 8 Paragraph 3; and

(ii)   an officer of inspector rank or above has inquired about the detainee's reasons for their change of mind and gives authority for the interview to proceed.

Confirmation of the detainee's agreement, their change of mind, the reasons for it if given and, subject to *paragraph 2.8,* the name of the authorising officer shall be recorded in the written interview record or the interview record made in accordance with the Code of Practice issued under Paragraph 3 of Schedule 8 to the Terrorism Act. See *Note 6H.* Note: In these circumstances the restriction on drawing adverse inferences from silence in *Annex C* will not apply because the detainee is allowed an opportunity to consult a solicitor if they wish.

6.8   If *paragraph 6.7(a)* applies, where the reason for authorising the delay ceases to apply, there may be no further delay in permitting the exercise of the right in the absence of a further authorisation unless *paragraph 6.7 (b), (c)* or *(d)* applies.

6.9   A detainee who has been permitted to consult a solicitor shall be entitled on request to have the solicitor present when they are interviewed unless one of the exceptions in *paragraph 6.7* applies.

6.10   The solicitor may only be required to leave the interview if their conduct is such that the interviewer is unable properly to put questions to the suspect. See *Notes 6C* and *6D*

6.11   If the interviewer considers a solicitor is acting in such a way, they will stop the interview and consult an officer not below superintendent rank, if one is readily available, and otherwise an officer not below inspector rank not connected with the investigation. After speaking to the solicitor, the officer consulted will decide if the interview should continue in the presence of that solicitor. If they decide it should not, the suspect will be given the opportunity to consult another solicitor before the interview continues and that solicitor given an opportunity to be present at the interview. See *Note 6D*

6.12   The removal of a solicitor from an interview is a serious step and, if it occurs, the officer of superintendent rank or above who took the decision will consider if the incident should be reported to the Law Society. If the decision to remove the solicitor has been taken by an officer below superintendent rank, the facts must be reported to an officer of superintendent rank or above who will similarly consider whether a report to the Law Society would be appropriate. When the solicitor concerned is a duty solicitor, the report should be both to the Law Society and to the Legal Services Commission.

6.13 'Solicitor' in this Code means:

- a solicitor who holds a current practising certificate

- an accredited or probationary representative included on the register of representatives maintained by the Legal Services Commission.

6.14 An accredited or probationary representative sent to provide advice by, and on behalf of, a solicitor shall be admitted to the police station for this purpose unless an officer of inspector rank or above considers such a visit will hinder the investigation and directs otherwise. Hindering the investigation does not include giving proper legal advice to a detainee as in *Note 6C*. Once admitted to the police station, *paragraphs 6.7* to *6.11* apply.

6.15 In exercising their discretion under *paragraph 6.14*, the officer should take into account in particular:

- whether:

  – the identity and status of an accredited or probationary representative have been satisfactorily established;

  – they are of suitable character to provide legal advice,

  – any other matters in any written letter of authorisation provided by the solicitor on whose behalf the person is attending the police station. See *Note 6E*

6.16 If the inspector refuses access to an accredited or probationary representative or a decision is taken that such a person should not be permitted to remain at an interview, the inspector must notify the solicitor on whose behalf the representative was acting and give them an opportunity to make alternative arrangements. The detainee must be informed and the custody record noted.

6.17 If a solicitor arrives at the station to see a particular person, that person must, unless *Annex B* applies, be so informed whether or not they are being interviewed and asked if they would like to see the solicitor. This applies even if the detainee has declined legal advice or, having requested it, subsequently agreed to be interviewed without receiving advice. The solicitor's attendance and the detainee's decision must be noted in the custody record.

(b) Documentation

6.18   Any request for legal advice and the action taken shall be recorded.

6.19   A record shall be made in the interview record if a detainee asks for legal advice and an interview is begun either in the absence of a solicitor or their representative, or they have been required to leave an interview.

Notes for guidance

6A   *If paragraph 6.7(b) applies, the officer should, if practicable, ask the solicitor for an estimate of how long it will take to come to the station and relate this to the time detention is permitted, the time of day (i.e. whether the rest period under paragraph 12.2 is imminent) and the requirements of other investigations. If the solicitor is on their way or is to set off immediately, it will not normally be appropriate to begin an interview before they arrive. If it appears necessary to begin an interview before the solicitor's arrival, they should be given an indication of how long the police would be able to wait so there is an opportunity to make arrangements for someone else to provide legal advice. Nothing within this section is intended to prevent police from ascertaining immediately after the arrest of an individual whether a threat to public safety exists (see paragraph 11.2).*

6B   *A detainee who asks for legal advice should be given an opportunity to consult a specific solicitor or another solicitor from that solicitor's firm or the duty solicitor. If advice is not available by these means, or they do not want to consult the duty solicitor, the detainee should be given an opportunity to choose a solicitor from a list of those willing to provide legal advice. If this solicitor is unavailable, they may choose up to two alternatives. If these attempts are unsuccessful, the custody officer has discretion to allow further attempts until a solicitor has been contacted and agrees to provide legal advice. Apart from carrying out these duties, an officer must not advise the suspect about any particular firm of solicitors.*

6C   *A detainee has a right to free legal advice and to be represented by a solicitor. The solicitor's only role in the police station is to protect and advance the legal rights of their client. On occasions this may require the solicitor to give advice which has the effect of the client avoiding giving evidence which strengthens a prosecution case. The solicitor may intervene in order to seek clarification, challenge an improper question to their client or the manner in which it is put, advise their client not to reply to particular questions, or if they wish to give their client further legal advice. Paragraph 6.9 only applies if the solicitor's approach or conduct prevents or unreasonably obstructs proper questions being put to the suspect or the suspect's response being recorded. Examples of unacceptable conduct include answering questions on a suspect's behalf or providing written replies for the suspect to quote.*

6D   An officer who takes the decision to exclude a solicitor must be in a position to satisfy the court the decision was properly made. In order to do this they may need to witness what is happening.

6E   If an officer of at least inspector rank considers a particular solicitor or firm of solicitors is persistently sending probationary representatives who are unsuited to provide legal advice, they should inform an officer of at least superintendent rank, who may wish to take the matter up with the Law Society.

6F   Subject to the constraints of Annex B, a solicitor may advise more than one client in an investigation if they wish. Any question of a conflict of interest is for the solicitor under their professional code of conduct. If, however, waiting for a solicitor to give advice to one client may lead to unreasonable delay to the interview with another, the provisions of paragraph 6.7(b) may apply.

6G   In addition to a poster in English, a poster or posters containing translations into Welsh, the main minority ethnic languages and the principal European languages should be displayed wherever they are likely to be helpful and it is practicable to do so.

6H   Paragraph 6.7(d) requires the authorisation of an officer of inspector rank or above to the continuation of an interview when a detainee who wanted legal advice changes their mind. It is permissible for such authorisation to be given over the telephone, if the authorising officer is able to satisfy themselves about the reason for the detainee's change of mind and is satisfied it is proper to continue the interview in those circumstances.

6I   Whenever a detainee exercises their right to legal advice by consulting or communicating with a solicitor, they must be allowed to do so in private. This right to consult or communicate in private is fundamental. Except as allowed by the Terrorism Act 2000, Schedule 8, paragraph 9, if the requirement for privacy is compromised because what is said or written by the detainee or solicitor for the purpose of giving and receiving legal advice is overheard, listened to, or read by others without the informed consent of the detainee, the right will effectively have been denied. When a detainee chooses to speak to a solicitor on the telephone, they should be allowed to do so in private unless a direction under Schedule 8, paragraph 9 of the Terrorism Act 2000 has been given or this is impractical because of the design and layout of the custody area, or the location of telephones. However, the normal expectation should be that facilities will be available, unless they are being used, at all police stations to enable detainees to speak in private to a solicitor either face to face or over the telephone.

6J   A detainee is not obliged to give reasons for declining legal advice and should not be pressed to do so.

7 Citizens of independent Commonwealth countries or foreign nationals

(a) Action

7.1 Any citizen of an independent Commonwealth country or a national of a foreign country, including the Republic of Ireland, may communicate at any time with the appropriate High Commission, Embassy or Consulate. The detainee must be informed as soon as practicable of:

- this right;

- their right, upon request, to have their High Commission, Embassy or Consulate told of their whereabouts and the grounds for their detention. Such a request should be acted upon as soon as practicable.

7.2 If a detainee is a citizen of a country with which a bilateral consular convention or agreement is in force requiring notification of arrest, the appropriate High Commission, Embassy or Consulate shall be informed as soon as practicable, subject to *paragraph 7.4*. The countries to which this applies as at 1 April 2003 are listed in *Annex F.*

7.3 Consular officers may visit one of their nationals in police detention to talk to them and, if required, to arrange for legal advice. Such visits shall take place out of the hearing of a police officer.

7.4 Notwithstanding the provisions of consular conventions, if the detainee is a political refugee whether for reasons of race, nationality, political opinion or religion, or is seeking political asylum, consular officers shall not be informed of the arrest of one of their nationals or given access or information about them except at the detainee's express request.

(b) Documentation

7.5 A record shall be made when a detainee is informed of their rights under this section and of any communications with a High Commission, Embassy or Consulate.

Note for guidance

7A The exercise of the rights in this section may not be interfered with even though Annex B applies.

8 Conditions of detention

(a) Action

8.1 So far as it is practicable, not more than one detainee should be detained in each cell.

8.2 Cells in use must be adequately heated, cleaned and ventilated. They must be adequately lit, subject to such dimming as is compatible with safety and security to allow people detained overnight to sleep. No additional restraints shall be used within a locked cell unless absolutely necessary and then only restraint equipment, approved for use in that force by the Chief Officer, which is reasonable and necessary in the circumstances having regard to the detainee's demeanour and with a view to ensuring their safety and the safety of others. If a detainee is deaf, mentally disordered or otherwise mentally vulnerable, particular care must be taken when deciding whether to use any form of approved restraints.

8.3 Blankets, mattresses, pillows and other bedding supplied shall be of a reasonable standard and in a clean and sanitary condition.

8.4 Access to toilet and washing facilities must be provided.

8.5 If it is necessary to remove a detainee's clothes for the purposes of investigation, for hygiene, health reasons or cleaning, replacement clothing of a reasonable standard of comfort and cleanliness shall be provided. A detainee may not be interviewed unless adequate clothing has been offered.

8.6 At least two light meals and one main meal should be offered in any 24 hour period. See *Note 8B.* Drinks should be provided at meal times and upon reasonable request between meals. Whenever necessary, advice shall be sought from the appropriate health care professional, see *Note 9A,* on medical and dietary matters. As far as practicable, meals provided shall offer a varied diet and meet any specific dietary needs or religious beliefs the detainee may have. Detainees should also be made aware that the meals offered meet such needs. The detainee may, at the custody officer's discretion, have meals supplied by their family or friends at their expense. See *Note 8A*

8.7 Brief outdoor exercise shall be offered daily if practicable. Where facilities exist, indoor exercise shall be offered as an alternative if outside conditions are such that a detainee can not be reasonably expected to take outdoor exercise (e.g., in cold or wet weather) or if requested by the detainee or for reasons of security, *see Note 8C.*

8.8 Where practicable, provision should be made for detainees to practice religious observance. Consideration should be given to providing a separate room which can be used as a prayer room. The supply of appropriate food and clothing, and suitable provision for prayer facilities, such as uncontaminated copies of religious books, should also be considered. *See Note 8D.*

8.9 A juvenile shall not be placed in a cell unless no other secure accommodation is available and the custody officer considers it is not practicable to supervise them if they are not placed in a cell or that cell provides more comfortable accommodation than

H

other secure accommodation in the station. A juvenile may not be placed in a cell with a detained adult.

8.10 Police stations should keep a reasonable supply of reading material available for detainees, including but not limited to, the main religious texts. *See Note 8D*. Detainees should be made aware that such material is available and reasonable requests for such material should be met as soon as practicable unless to do so would:

(i) interfere with the investigation; or

(ii) prevent or delay an officer from discharging his statutory duties, or those in this Code.

If such a request is refused on the grounds of (i) or (ii) above, this should be noted in the custody record and met as soon as possible after those grounds cease to apply.

(b) Documentation

8.11 A record must be kept of replacement clothing and meals offered.

8.12 The use of any restraints on a detainee whilst in a cell, the reasons for it and, if appropriate, the arrangements for enhanced supervision of the detainee whilst so restrained, shall be recorded. See *paragraph 3.9*

Notes for guidance

8A In deciding whether to allow meals to be supplied by family or friends, the custody officer is entitled to take account of the risk of items being concealed in any food or package and the officer's duties and responsibilities under food handling legislation. If an officer needs to examine food or other items supplied by family and friends before deciding whether they can be given to the detainee, he should inform the person who has brought the item to the police station of this and the reasons for doing so.

8B Meals should, so far as practicable, be offered at recognised meal times, or at other times that take account of when the detainee last had a meal.

8C In light of the potential for detaining individuals for extended periods of time, the overriding principle should be to accommodate a period of exercise, except where to do so would hinder the investigation, delay the detainee's release or charge, or it is declined by the detainee.

8D Police forces should consult with representatives of the main religious communities to ensure the provision for religious observance is adequate, and to seek advice on the appropriate storage and handling of religious texts or other religious items.

9 Care and treatment of detained persons

(a) General

9.1 Notwithstanding other requirements for medical attention as set out in this section, detainees who are held for more than 96 hours must be visited by a healthcare professional at least once every 24 hours.

9.2 Nothing in this section prevents the police from calling the police surgeon or, if appropriate, some other health care professional, to examine a detainee for the purposes of obtaining evidence relating to any offence in which the detainee is suspected of being involved. See *Note 9A*

9.3 If a complaint is made by, or on behalf of, a detainee about their treatment since their arrest, or it comes to notice that a detainee may have been treated improperly, a report must be made as soon as practicable to an officer of inspector rank or above not connected with the investigation. If the matter concerns a possible assault or the possibility of the unnecessary or unreasonable use of force, an appropriate health care professional must also be called as soon as practicable.

9.4 Detainees should be visited at least every hour. If no reasonably foreseeable risk was identified in a risk assessment, see *paragraphs 3.6 – 3.10*, there is no need to wake a sleeping detainee. Those suspected of being intoxicated through drink or drugs or having swallowed drugs, see *Note 9C*, or whose level of consciousness causes concern must, subject to any clinical directions given by the appropriate health care professional, see *paragraph 9.15*:

- be visited and roused at least every half hour

- have their condition assessed as in *Annex H*

- and clinical treatment arranged if appropriate

See *Notes 9B, 9C* and *9G*

9.5 When arrangements are made to secure clinical attention for a detainee, the custody officer must make sure all relevant information which might assist in the treatment of the detainee's condition is made available to the responsible health care professional. This applies whether or not the health care professional asks for such information. Any officer or police staff with relevant information must inform the custody officer as soon as practicable.

H

(b)   Clinical treatment and attention

9.6   The custody officer must make sure a detainee receives appropriate clinical attention as soon as reasonably practicable if the person:

(a)   appears to be suffering from physical illness; or

(b)   is injured; or

(c)   appears to be suffering from a mental disorder; or

(d)   appears to need clinical attention

9.7   This applies even if the detainee makes no request for clinical attention and whether or not they have already received clinical attention elsewhere. If the need for attention appears urgent, e.g. when indicated as in *Annex H*, the nearest available health care professional or an ambulance must be called immediately.

9.8   The custody officer must also consider the need for clinical attention as set out in *Note 9C* in relation to those suffering the effects of alcohol or drugs.

9.9   If it appears to the custody officer, or they are told, that a person brought to a station under arrest may be suffering from an infectious disease or condition, the custody officer must take reasonable steps to safeguard the health of the detainee and others at the station. In deciding what action to take, advice must be sought from an appropriate health care professional. See *Note 9D*. The custody officer has discretion to isolate the person and their property until clinical directions have been obtained.

9.10   If a detainee requests a clinical examination, an appropriate health care professional must be called as soon as practicable to assess the detainee's clinical needs. If a safe and appropriate care plan cannot be provided, the police surgeon's advice must be sought. The detainee may also be examined by a medical practitioner of their choice at their expense.

9.11   If a detainee is required to take or apply any medication in compliance with clinical directions prescribed before their detention, the custody officer must consult the appropriate health care professional before the use of the medication. Subject to the restrictions in *paragraph 9.12*, the custody officer is responsible for the safekeeping of any medication and for making sure the detainee is given the opportunity to take or apply prescribed or approved medication. Any such consultation and its outcome shall be noted in the custody record.

9.12   No police officer may administer or supervise the self-administration of medically prescribed controlled drugs of the types and forms listed in the Misuse of Drugs Regulations 2001, Schedule 2 or 3. A detainee may only self-administer such drugs under the personal supervision of the registered medical practitioner authorising their use. Drugs listed in Schedule 4 or 5 may be distributed by the custody officer for self-administration if they have consulted the registered medical practitioner authorising their use, this may be done by telephone, and both parties are satisfied self-administration will not expose the detainee, police officers or anyone else to the risk of harm or injury.

9.13 When appropriate health care professionals administer drugs or other medications, or supervise their self-administration, it must be within current medicines legislation and the scope of practice as determined by their relevant professional body.

9.14 If a detainee has in their possession, or claims to need, medication relating to a heart condition, diabetes, epilepsy or a condition of comparable potential seriousness then, even though *paragraph 9.6* may not apply, the advice of the appropriate health care professional must be obtained.

9.15 Whenever the appropriate health care professional is called in accordance with this section to examine or treat a detainee, the custody officer shall ask for their opinion about:

- any risks or problems which police need to take into account when making decisions about the detainee's continued detention;

- when to carry out an interview if applicable; and

- the need for safeguards.

9.16 When clinical directions are given by the appropriate health care professional, whether orally or in writing, and the custody officer has any doubts or is in any way uncertain about any aspect of the directions, the custody officer shall ask for clarification. It is particularly important that directions concerning the frequency of visits are clear, precise and capable of being implemented. See *Note 9E*.

(c) Documentation

9.17 A record must be made in the custody record of:

(a) the arrangements made for an examination by an appropriate health care professional under *paragraph 9.3* and of any complaint reported under that paragraph together with any relevant remarks by the custody officer;

(b) any arrangements made in accordance with *paragraph 9.6*;

(c) any request for a clinical examination under *paragraph 9.10* and any arrangements made in response;

(d)   the injury, ailment, condition or other reason which made it necessary to make the arrangements in (*a*) to (*c*), see *Note 9F;*

(e)   any clinical directions and advice, including any further clarifications, given to police by a health care professional concerning the care and treatment of the detainee in connection with any of the arrangements made in (*a*) to (*c*), see *Note 9E;*

(f)   if applicable, the responses received when attempting to rouse a person using the procedure in *Annex H,* see *Note 9G.*

9.18   If a health care professional does not record their clinical findings in the custody record, the record must show where they are recorded. See *Note 9F.* However, information which is necessary to custody staff to ensure the effective ongoing care and well being of the detainee must be recorded openly in the custody record, see *paragraph 3.8* and *Annex G, paragraph 7.*

9.19   Subject to the requirements of *Section 4*, the custody record shall include:

•   a record of all medication a detainee has in their possession on arrival at the police station;

•   a note of any such medication they claim to need but do not have with them.

Notes for guidance

9A   A 'health care professional' means a clinically qualified person working within the scope of practice as determined by their relevant professional body. Whether a health care professional is 'appropriate' depends on the circumstances of the duties they carry out at the time.

9B   Whenever possible juveniles and mentally vulnerable detainees should be visited more frequently.

9C   A detainee who appears drunk or behaves abnormally may be suffering from illness, the effects of drugs or may have sustained injury, particularly a head injury which is not apparent. A detainee needing or dependent on certain drugs, including alcohol, may experience harmful effects within a short time of being deprived of their supply. In these circumstances, when there is any doubt, police should always act urgently to call an appropriate health care professional or an ambulance. Paragraph 9.6 does not apply to minor ailments or injuries which do not need attention. However, all such ailments or injuries must be recorded in the custody record and any doubt must be resolved in favour of calling the appropriate health care professional.

9D *It is important to respect a person's right to privacy and information about their health must be kept confidential and only disclosed with their consent or in accordance with clinical advice when it is necessary to protect the detainee's health or that of others who come into contact with them.*

9E *The custody officer should always seek to clarify directions that the detainee requires constant observation or supervision and should ask the appropriate health care professional to explain precisely what action needs to be taken to implement such directions.*

9F *Paragraphs 9.17 and 9.18 do not require any information about the cause of any injury, ailment or condition to be recorded on the custody record if it appears capable of providing evidence of an offence.*

9G *The purpose of recording a person's responses when attempting to rouse them using the procedure in Annex H is to enable any change in the individual's consciousness level to be noted and clinical treatment arranged if appropriate.*

10   Cautions

(a)   When a caution must be given

10.1 A person whom there are grounds to suspect of an offence, see *Note 10A*, must be cautioned before any questions about an offence, or further questions if the answers provide the grounds for suspicion, are put to them if either the suspect's answers or silence, (i.e. failure or refusal to answer or answer satisfactorily) may be given in evidence to a court in a prosecution.

10.2 A person who is arrested, or further arrested, must be informed at the time, or as soon as practicable thereafter, that they are under arrest and the grounds for their arrest, see paragraph 3.4, *Note 3G* and *Note 10B*.

10.3 As per *section 3* of PACE Code G, a person who is arrested, or further arrested, must also be cautioned unless:

(a)   it is impracticable to do so by reason of their condition or behaviour at the time;

(b)   they have already been cautioned immediately prior to arrest as in *paragraph 10.1*.

(b)   Terms of the cautions

10.4 The caution which must be given on:

(a)   arrest;

(b) all other occasions before a person is charged or informed they may be prosecuted, see *PACE Code C*, section 16.

should, unless the restriction on drawing adverse inferences from silence applies, see *Annex C*, be in the following terms:

"You do not have to say anything. But it may harm your defence if you do not mention when questioned something which you later rely on in Court. Anything you do say may be given in evidence."

See *Note 10F*

10.5 *Annex C, paragraph 2* sets out the alternative terms of the caution to be used when the restriction on drawing adverse inferences from silence applies.

10.6 Minor deviations from the words of any caution given in accordance with this Code do not constitute a breach of this Code, provided the sense of the relevant caution is preserved. See *Note 10C*

10.7 After any break in questioning under caution, the person being questioned must be made aware they remain under caution. If there is any doubt the relevant caution should be given again in full when the interview resumes. See *Note 10D*

10.8 When, despite being cautioned, a person fails to co-operate or to answer particular questions which may affect their immediate treatment, the person should be informed of any relevant consequences and that those consequences are not affected by the caution. Examples are when a person's refusal to provide:

- their name and address when charged may make them liable to detention;

- particulars and information in accordance with a statutory requirement

(c) Special warnings under the Criminal Justice and Public Order Act 1994, sections 36 and 37

10.9 When a suspect interviewed at a police station or authorised place of detention after arrest fails or refuses to answer certain questions, or to answer satisfactorily, after due warning, see *Note 10E*, a court or jury may draw such inferences as appear proper under the Criminal Justice and Public Order Act 1994, sections 36 and 37. Such inferences may only be drawn when:

(a) the restriction on drawing adverse inferences from silence, see *Annex C,* does not apply; and

116

(b)   the suspect is arrested by a constable and fails or refuses to account for any objects, marks or substances, or marks on such objects found:

- on their person;

- in or on their clothing or footwear;

- otherwise in their possession; or

- in the place they were arrested;

(c)   the arrested suspect was found by a constable at a place at or about the time the offence for which that officer has arrested them is alleged to have been committed, and the suspect fails or refuses to account for their presence there.

When the restriction on drawing adverse inferences from silence applies, the suspect may still be asked to account for any of the matters in (*b*) or (*c*) but the special warning described in *paragraph 10.10* will not apply and must not be given.

10.10 For an inference to be drawn when a suspect fails or refuses to answer a question about one of these matters or to answer it satisfactorily, the suspect must first be told in ordinary language:

(a)   what offence is being investigated;

(b)   what fact they are being asked to account for;

(c)   this fact may be due to them taking part in the commission of the offence;

(d)   a court may draw a proper inference if they fail or refuse to account for this fact;

(e)   a record is being made of the interview and it may be given in evidence if they are brought to trial.

(d)   *Juveniles and persons who are mentally disordered or otherwise mentally vulnerable*

10.11 If a juvenile or a person who is mentally disordered or otherwise mentally vulnerable is cautioned in the absence of the appropriate adult, the caution must be repeated in the adult's presence.

(e)   *Documentation*

10.12 A record shall be made when a caution is given under this section, either in the interviewer's pocket book or in the interview record.

H

H

Notes for guidance

10A   There must be some reasonable, objective grounds for the suspicion, based on known facts or information which are relevant to the likelihood the offence has been committed and the person to be questioned committed it.

10B   An arrested person must be given sufficient information to enable them to understand that they have been deprived of their liberty and the reason they have been arrested, e.g. when a person is arrested on suspicion of committing an offence they must be informed of the suspected offence's nature, when and where it was committed see Note 3G. The suspect must also be informed of the reason or reasons why the arrest is considered necessary. Vague or technical language should be avoided.

10C   If it appears a person does not understand the caution, the person giving it should explain it in their own words.

10D   It may be necessary to show to the court that nothing occurred during an interview break or between interviews which influenced the suspect's recorded evidence. After a break in an interview or at the beginning of a subsequent interview, the interviewing officer should summarise the reason for the break and confirm this with the suspect.

10E   The Criminal Justice and Public Order Act 1994, sections 36 and 37 apply only to suspects who have been arrested by a constable or Customs and Excise officer and are given the relevant warning by the police or customs officer who made the arrest or who is investigating the offence. They do not apply to any interviews with suspects who have not been arrested.

10F   Nothing in this Code requires a caution to be given or repeated when informing a person not under arrest they may be prosecuted for an offence. However, a court will not be able to draw any inferences under the Criminal Justice and Public Order Act 1994, section 34, if the person was not cautioned.

11   Interviews – general

(a)   Action

11.1   An interview in this Code is the questioning of a person arrested on suspicion of being a terrorist which, under *paragraph 10.1*, must be carried out under caution. Whenever a person is interviewed they must be informed of the grounds for arrest *see Note 3G*.

11.2   Following a decision to arrest a suspect, they must not be interviewed about the relevant offence except at a place designated for detention under Schedule 8 paragraph 1 of the Terrorism Act 2000, unless the consequent delay would be likely to:

(a)   lead to:

- interference with, or harm to, evidence connected with an offence;

- interference with, or physical harm to, other people; or

- serious loss of, or damage to, property;

(b)   lead to alerting other people suspected of committing an offence but not yet arrested for it; or

(c)   hinder the recovery of property obtained in consequence of the commission of an offence.

Interviewing in any of these circumstances shall cease once the relevant risk has been averted or the necessary questions have been put in order to attempt to avert that risk.

11.3   Immediately prior to the commencement or re-commencement of any interview at a designated place of detention, the interviewer should remind the suspect of their entitlement to free legal advice and that the interview can be delayed for legal advice to be obtained, unless one of the exceptions in *paragraph 6.7* applies. It is the interviewer's responsibility to make sure all reminders are recorded in the interview record.

11.4   At the beginning of an interview the interviewer, after cautioning the suspect, see *section 10*, shall put to them any significant statement or silence which occurred in the presence and hearing of a police officer or other police staff before the start of the interview and which have not been put to the suspect in the course of a previous interview. See *Note 11A*. The interviewer shall ask the suspect whether they confirm or deny that earlier statement or silence and if they want to add anything.

11.5   A significant statement is one which appears capable of being used in evidence against the suspect, in particular a direct admission of guilt. A significant silence is a failure or refusal to answer a question or answer satisfactorily when under caution, which might, allowing for the restriction on drawing adverse inferences from silence, see *Annex C*, give rise to an inference under the Criminal Justice and Public Order Act 1994, Part III.

11.6   No interviewer may try to obtain answers or elicit a statement by the use of oppression. Except as in *paragraph 10.8*, no interviewer shall indicate, except to answer a direct question, what action will be taken by the police if the person being questioned answers questions, makes a statement or refuses to do either. If the person asks directly what action will be taken if they answer questions, make a statement or refuse to do either, the interviewer may inform them what action the police propose to take provided that action is itself proper and warranted.

11.7   The interview or further interview of a person about an offence with which that person has not been charged or for which they have not been informed they may be prosecuted, must cease when:

(a)   the officer in charge of the investigation is satisfied all the questions they consider relevant to obtaining accurate and reliable information about the offence have been put to the suspect, this includes allowing the suspect an opportunity to give an innocent explanation and asking questions to test if the explanation is accurate and reliable, e.g. to clear up ambiguities or clarify what the suspect said;

(b)   the officer in charge of the investigation has taken account of any other available evidence; and

(c)   the officer in charge of the investigation, or in the case of a detained suspect, the custody officer, see *PACE Code C paragraph 16.1*, reasonably believes there is sufficient evidence to provide a realistic prospect of conviction for that offence. See *Note 11B*

(b)   Interview records

11.8   Interview records should be made in accordance with the Code of Practice issued under Schedule 8 Paragraph 3 to the Terrorism Act where the interview takes place at a designated place of detention.

(c)   Juveniles and mentally disordered or otherwise mentally vulnerable people

11.9   A juvenile or person who is mentally disordered or otherwise mentally vulnerable must not be interviewed regarding their involvement or suspected involvement in a criminal offence or offences, or asked to provide or sign a written statement under caution or record of interview, in the absence of the appropriate adult unless *paragraphs 11.2, 11.11* to *11.13* apply. See *Note 11C*

11.10 If an appropriate adult is present at an interview, they shall be informed:

- they are not expected to act simply as an observer; and

- the purpose of their presence is to:

  - advise the person being interviewed;

  - observe whether the interview is being conducted properly and fairly;

  - facilitate communication with the person being interviewed.

The appropriate adult may be required to leave the interview if their conduct is such that the interviewer is unable properly to put questions to the suspect. This will include situations where the appropriate adult's approach or conduct prevents or unreasonably obstructs proper questions being put to the suspect or the suspect's responses being recorded. If the interviewer considers an appropriate adult is acting in such a way, they will stop the interview and consult an officer not below superintendent rank, if one is readily available, and otherwise an officer not below inspector rank not connected with the investigation. After speaking to the appropriate adult, the officer consulted will decide if the interview should continue without the attendance of that appropriate adult. If they decide it should not, another appropriate adult should be obtained before the interview continues, unless the provisions of paragraph 11.11 below apply.

H

(d)   *Vulnerable suspects – urgent interviews at police stations*

11.11 The following persons may not be interviewed unless an officer of superintendent rank or above considers delay will lead to the consequences in *paragraph 11.2(a)* to *(c)*, and is satisfied the interview would not significantly harm the person's physical or mental state (see Annex G):

(a) a juvenile or person who is mentally disordered or otherwise mentally vulnerable if at the time of the interview the appropriate adult is not present;

(b) anyone other than in (a) who at the time of the interview appears unable to:

- appreciate the significance of questions and their answers; or

- understand what is happening because of the effects of drink, drugs or any illness, ailment or condition;

(c) a person who has difficulty understanding English or has a hearing disability, if at the time of the interview an interpreter is not present.

11.12 These interviews may not continue once sufficient information has been obtained to avert the consequences in *paragraph 11.2(a)* to *(c)*.

11.13 A record shall be made of the grounds for any decision to interview a person under *paragraph 11.11*.

H

Notes for guidance

11A *Paragraph 11.4 does not prevent the interviewer from putting significant statements and silences to a suspect again at a later stage or a further interview.*

11B *The Criminal Procedure and Investigations Act 1996 Code of Practice, paragraph 3.4 states 'In conducting an investigation, the investigator should pursue all reasonable lines of enquiry, whether these point towards or away from the suspect. What is reasonable will depend on the particular circumstances.' Interviewers should keep this in mind when deciding what questions to ask in an interview.*

11C *Although juveniles or people who are mentally disordered or otherwise mentally vulnerable are often capable of providing reliable evidence, they may, without knowing or wishing to do so, be particularly prone in certain circumstances to provide information that may be unreliable, misleading or self-incriminating. Special care should always be taken when questioning such a person, and the appropriate adult should be involved if there is any doubt about a person's age, mental state or capacity. Because of the risk of unreliable evidence it is also important to obtain corroboration of any facts admitted whenever possible.*

11D *Consideration should be given to the effect of extended detention on a detainee and any subsequent information they provide, especially if it relates to information on matters that they have failed to provide previously in response to similar questioning see Annex G.*

11E *Significant statements described in paragraph 11.4 will always be relevant to the offence and must be recorded. When a suspect agrees to read records of interviews and other comments and sign them as correct, they should be asked to endorse the record with, e.g. 'I agree that this is a correct record of what was said' and add their signature. If the suspect does not agree with the record, the interviewer should record the details of any disagreement and ask the suspect to read these details and sign them to the effect that they accurately reflect their disagreement. Any refusal to sign should be recorded.*

12   Interviews in police stations

(a)   Action

12.1 If a police officer wants to interview or conduct enquiries which require the presence of a detainee, the custody officer is responsible for deciding whether to deliver the detainee into the officer's custody.

12.2 Except as below, in any period of 24 hours a detainee must be allowed a continuous period of at least 8 hours for rest, free from questioning, travel or any interruption in connection with the investigation concerned. This period should normally be at night or other appropriate time which takes account of when the detainee last slept or rested. If a detainee is arrested at a police station after going there voluntarily, the period of 24 hours runs from the time of their arrest (or, if a person was being detained under TACT Schedule 7 when arrested, from the time at which the examination under Schedule 7 began) and not the time of arrival at the police station. The period may not be interrupted or delayed, except:

(a)   when there are reasonable grounds for believing not delaying or interrupting the period would:

    (i)   involve a risk of harm to people or serious loss of, or damage to, property;

    (ii)   delay unnecessarily the person's release from custody;

    (iii)   otherwise prejudice the outcome of the investigation;

(b)   at the request of the detainee, their appropriate adult or legal representative;

(c)   when a delay or interruption is necessary in order to:

    (i)   comply with the legal obligations and duties arising under *section 14*;

    (ii)   to take action required under *section 9* or in accordance with medical advice.

If the period is interrupted in accordance with *(a)*, a fresh period must be allowed. Interruptions under *(b)* and *(c)*, do not require a fresh period to be allowed.

12.3   Before a detainee is interviewed the custody officer, in consultation with the officer in charge of the investigation and appropriate health care professionals as necessary, shall assess whether the detainee is fit enough to be interviewed. This means determining and considering the risks to the detainee's physical and mental state if the interview took place and determining what safeguards are needed to allow the interview to take place. The custody officer shall not allow a detainee to be interviewed if the custody officer considers it would cause significant harm to the detainee's physical or mental state. Vulnerable suspects listed at *paragraph 11.11* shall be treated as always being at some risk during an interview and these persons may not be interviewed except in accordance with *paragraphs 11.11* to *11.13*.

12.4   As far as practicable interviews shall take place in interview rooms which are adequately heated, lit and ventilated.

12.5   A suspect whose detention without charge has been authorised under TACT Schedule 8, because the detention is necessary for an interview to obtain evidence of the offence

H

for which they have been arrested, may choose not to answer questions but police do not require the suspect's consent or agreement to interview them for this purpose. If a suspect takes steps to prevent themselves being questioned or further questioned, e.g. by refusing to leave their cell to go to a suitable interview room or by trying to leave the interview room, they shall be advised their consent or agreement to interview is not required. The suspect shall be cautioned as in *section 10*, and informed if they fail or refuse to co-operate, the interview may take place in the cell and that their failure or refusal to co-operate may be given in evidence. The suspect shall then be invited to co-operate and go into the interview room.

12.6　People being questioned or making statements shall not be required to stand.

12.7　Before the interview commences each interviewer shall, subject to the qualification at *paragraph 2.8,* identify themselves and any other persons present to the interviewee.

12.8　Breaks from interviewing should be made at recognised meal times or at other times that take account of when an interviewee last had a meal. Short refreshment breaks shall be provided at approximately two hour intervals, subject to the interviewer's discretion to delay a break if there are reasonable grounds for believing it would:

(i)　involve a:

- risk of harm to people;

- serious loss of, or damage to, property;

(ii)　unnecessarily delay the detainee's release;

(iii)　otherwise prejudice the outcome of the investigation.

See *Note 12B*

12.9　During extended periods where no interviews take place, because of the need to gather further evidence or analyse existing evidence, detainees and their legal representative shall be informed that the investigation into the relevant offence remains ongoing. If practicable, the detainee and legal representative should also be made aware in general terms of any reasons for long gaps between interviews. Consideration should be given to allowing visits, more frequent exercise, or for reading or writing materials to be offered *see paragraph 5.4, section 8* and *Note 12C*.

12.10 If during the interview a complaint is made by or on behalf of the interviewee concerning the provisions of this Code, the interviewer should:

(i)　record it in the interview record;

(ii)   inform the custody officer, who is then responsible for dealing with it as in *section 9*.

(b)   Documentation

12.11 A record must be made of the:

- time a detainee is not in the custody of the custody officer, and why

- reason for any refusal to deliver the detainee out of that custody

12.12 A record shall be made of:

(a)   the reasons it was not practicable to use an interview room; and

(b)   any action taken as in *paragraph 12.5*.

The record shall be made on the custody record or in the interview record for action taken whilst an interview record is being kept, with a brief reference to this effect in the custody record.

12.13 Any decision to delay a break in an interview must be recorded, with reasons, in the interview record.

12.14 All written statements made at police stations under caution shall be written on forms provided for the purpose.

12.15 All written statements made under caution shall be taken in accordance with *Annex D*. Before a person makes a written statement under caution at a police station they shall be reminded about the right to legal advice. See *Note 12A*

Notes for guidance

12A   It is not normally necessary to ask for a written statement if the interview was recorded in writing and the record signed in accordance with the Code of Practice issued under TACT Schedule 8 Paragraph 3. Statements under caution should normally be taken in these circumstances only at the person's express wish. A person may however be asked if they want to make such a statement.

12B   Meal breaks should normally last at least 45 minutes and shorter breaks after two hours should last at least 15 minutes. If the interviewer delays a break in accordance with paragraph 12.8 and prolongs the interview, a longer break should be provided. If there is a short interview, and another short interview is contemplated, the length of the break may be reduced if there are reasonable grounds to believe this is necessary to avoid any of the consequences in paragraph 12.8(i) to (iii).

12C   Consideration should be given to the matters referred to in paragraph 12.9 after a period of over 24 hours without questioning. This is to ensure that extended periods of detention without an indication that the investigation remains ongoing do not contribute to a deterioration of the detainee's well-being.

13   Interpreters

(a)   General

13.1   Chief officers are responsible for making sure appropriate arrangements are in place for provision of suitably qualified interpreters for people who:

- are deaf;

- do not understand English.

Whenever possible, interpreters should be drawn from the National Register of Public Service Interpreters (NRPSI) or the Council for the Advancement of Communication with Deaf People (CACDP) Directory of British Sign Language/English Interpreters.

(b)   Foreign languages

13.2   Unless *paragraphs 11.2, 11.11 to 11.13* apply, a person must not be interviewed in the absence of a person capable of interpreting if:

(a)   they have difficulty understanding English;

(b)   the interviewer cannot speak the person's own language;

(c)   the person wants an interpreter present.

13.3   The interviewer shall make sure the interpreter makes a note of the interview at the time in the person's language for use in the event of the interpreter being called to give evidence, and certifies its accuracy. The interviewer should allow sufficient time for the interpreter to note each question and answer after each is put, given and interpreted. The person should be allowed to read the record or have it read to them and sign it as correct or indicate the respects in which they consider it inaccurate. If the interview is audibly recorded or visually recorded with sound, the Code of Practice issued under paragraph 3 of Schedule 8 to the Terrorism Act 2000 will apply.

13.4   In the case of a person making a statement to a police officer or other police staff other than in English:

(a)   the interpreter shall record the statement in the language it is made;

(b)   the person shall be invited to sign it;

(c)   an official English translation shall be made in due course.

(c)   Deaf people and people with speech difficulties

13.5   If a person appears to be deaf or there is doubt about their hearing or speaking ability, they must not be interviewed in the absence of an interpreter unless they agree in writing to being interviewed without one or *paragraphs 11.2, 11.11 to 11.13* apply.

13.6   An interpreter should also be called if a juvenile is interviewed and the parent or guardian present as the appropriate adult appears to be deaf or there is doubt about their hearing or speaking ability, unless they agree in writing to the interview proceeding without one or *paragraphs 11.2, 11.11 to 11.13* apply.

13.7   The interviewer shall make sure the interpreter is allowed to read the interview record and certify its accuracy in the event of the interpreter being called to give evidence. If the interview is audibly recorded or visually recorded, the Code of Practice issued under TACT Schedule 8 Paragraph 3 will apply.

(d)   Additional rules for detained persons

13.8   All reasonable attempts should be made to make the detainee understand that interpreters will be provided at public expense.

13.9   If *paragraph 6.1* applies and the detainee cannot communicate with the solicitor because of language, hearing or speech difficulties, an interpreter must be called. The interpreter may not be a police officer or any other police staff when interpretation is needed for the purposes of obtaining legal advice. In all other cases a police officer or other police staff may only interpret if the detainee and the appropriate adult, if applicable, give their agreement in writing or if the interview is audibly recorded or visually recorded as in the Code of Practice issued under TACT Schedule 8 Paragraph 3.

13.10   When the custody officer cannot establish effective communication with a person charged with an offence who appears deaf or there is doubt about their ability to hear, speak or to understand English, arrangements must be made as soon as practicable for an interpreter to explain the offence and any other information given by the custody officer.

(e)   Documentation

13.11   Action taken to call an interpreter under this section and any agreement to be interviewed in the absence of an interpreter must be recorded.

H

14 Reviews and Extensions of Detention

(a) Reviews and Extensions of Detention

14.1 The powers and duties of the review officer are in the Terrorism Act 2000, Schedule 8, Part II. See *Notes 14A* and *14B*. A review officer should carry out his duties at the police station where the detainee is held, and be allowed such access to the detainee as is necessary for him to exercise those duties.

14.2 For the purposes of reviewing a person's detention, no officer shall put specific questions to the detainee:

- regarding their involvement in any offence; or

- in respect of any comments they may make:

  - when given the opportunity to make representations; or

  - in response to a decision to keep them in detention or extend the maximum period of detention.

Such an exchange could constitute an interview as in *paragraph 11.1* and would be subject to the associated safeguards in *section 11* and, in respect of a person who has been charged see *PACE Code C Section 16.8.*

14.3 If detention is necessary for longer than 48 hours, a police officer of at least superintendent rank, or a Crown Prosecutor may apply for warrants of further detention under the Terrorism Act 2000, Schedule 8, Part III.

14.4 When an application for a warrant of further or extended detention is sought under Paragraph 29 or 36 of Schedule 8, the detained person and their representative must be informed of their rights in respect of the application. These include:

a) the right to a written or oral notice of the warrant See *Note 14G.*

b) the right to make oral or written representations to the judicial authority about the application.

c) the right to be present and legally represented at the hearing of the application, unless specifically excluded by the judicial authority.

d) their right to free legal advice (see section 6 of this Code).

(b)   Transfer of detained persons to Prison

14.5   Where a warrant is issued which authorises detention beyond a period of 14 days from the time of arrest (or if a person was being detained under TACT Schedule 7, from the time at which the examination under Schedule 7 began), the detainee must be transferred from detention in a police station to detention in a designated prison as soon as is practicable, unless:

a)   the detainee specifically requests to remain in detention at a police station and that request can be accommodated, or

b)   there are reasonable grounds to believe that transferring a person to a prison would:

i)   significantly hinder a terrorism investigation;

ii)   delay charging of the detainee or his release from custody, or

iii)   otherwise prevent the investigation from being conducted diligently and expeditiously.

If any of the grounds in (b)(i) to (iii) above are relied upon, these must be presented to the judicial authority as part of the application for the warrant that would extend detention beyond a period of 14 days from the time of arrest (or if a person was being detained under TACT Schedule 7, from the time at which the examination under Schedule 7 began) *See Note 14.1*

14.6   If a person remains in detention at a police station under a warrant of further detention as described at section 14.5, they must be transferred to a prison as soon as practicable after the grounds at (b)(i) to (iii) of that section cease to apply.

14.7   Police should maintain an agreement with the National Offender Management Service (NOMS) that stipulates named prisons to which individuals may be transferred under this section. This should be made with regard to ensuring detainees are moved to the most suitable prison for the purposes of the investigation and their welfare, and should include provision for the transfer of male, female and juvenile detainees. Police should ensure that the Governor of a prison to which they intend to transfer a detainee is given reasonable notice of this. Where practicable, this should be no later than the point at which a warrant is applied for that would take the period of detention beyond 14 days.

14.8   Following a detained person's transfer to a designated prison, their detention will be governed by the terms of Schedule 8 and Prison Rules, and this Code of Practice will not apply during any period that the person remains in prison detention. The Code will once more apply if a detained person is transferred back from prison detention to police

H

detention. In order to enable the Governor to arrange for the production of the detainee back into police custody, police should give notice to the Governor of the relevant prison as soon as possible of any decision to transfer a detainee from prison back to a police station. Any transfer between a prison and a police station should be conducted by police, and this Code will be applicable during the period of transit See *Note 14K*. A detainee should only remain in police custody having been transferred back from a prison, for as long as is necessary for the purpose of the investigation.

14.9 The investigating team and custody officer should provide as much information as necessary to enable the relevant prison authorities to provide appropriate facilities to detain an individual. This should include, but not be limited to:

i)   medical assessments

ii)   security and risk assessments

iii)   details of the detained person's legal representatives

iv)   details of any individuals from whom the detained person has requested visits, or who have requested to visit the detained person.

14.10 Where a detainee is to be transferred to prison, the custody officer should inform the detainee's legal adviser beforehand that the transfer is to take place (including the name of the prison). The custody officer should also make all reasonable attempts to inform:

- family or friends who have been informed previously of the detainee's detention; and

- the person who was initially informed of the detainee's detention as at *paragraph 5.1*.

(c)   Documentation

14.11 It is the responsibility of the officer who gives any reminders as at *paragraph 14.4*, to ensure that these are noted in the custody record, as well any comments made by the detained person upon being told of those rights.

14.12 The grounds for, and extent of, any delay in conducting a review shall be recorded.

14.13 Any written representations shall be retained.

14.14 A record shall be made as soon as practicable about the outcome of each review or determination whether to extend the maximum detention period without charge or an application for a warrant of further detention or its extension.

14.15 Any decision not to transfer a detained person to a designated prison under paragraph *14.5*, must be recorded, along with the reasons for this decision. If a request under paragraph *14.5(a)* is not accommodated, the reasons for this should also be recorded.

Notes for guidance

14A   *TACT Schedule 8 Part II sets out the procedures for review of detention up to 48 hours from the time of arrest under TACT section 41 (or if a person was being detained under TACT Schedule 7, from the time at which the examination under Schedule 7 began). These include provisions for the requirement to review detention, postponing a review, grounds for continued detention, designating a review officer, representations, rights of the detained person and keeping a record. The review officer's role ends after a warrant has been issued for extension of detention under Part III of Schedule 8.*

14B   *Section 24(1) of the Terrorism Act 2006, amended the grounds contained within the 2000 Act on which a review officer may authorise continued detention. Continued detention may be authorised if it is necessary-*

a)   *to obtain relevant evidence whether by questioning him or otherwise*

b)   *to preserve relevant evidence*

c)   *while awaiting the result of an examination or analysis of relevant evidence*

d)   *for the examination or analysis of anything with a view to obtaining relevant evidence*

e)   *pending a decision to apply to the Secretary of State for a deportation notice to be served on the detainee, the making of any such application, or the consideration of any such application by the Secretary of State*

f)   *pending a decision to charge the detainee with an offence.*

14C   *Applications for warrants to extend detention beyond 48 hours, may be made for periods of 7 days at a time (initially under TACT Schedule 8 paragraph 29, and extensions thereafter under TACT Schedule 8, Paragraph 36), up to a maximum period of 28 days from the time of arrest (or if a person was being detained under TACT Schedule 7, from the time at which the examination under Schedule 7 began). Applications may be made for shorter periods than 7 days, which must be specified. The judicial authority may also substitute a shorter period if he feels a period of 7 days is inappropriate.*

14D   *Unless Note 14F applies, applications for warrants that would take the total period of detention up to 14 days or less should be made to a judicial authority, meaning a*

H

District Judge (Magistrates' Court) designated by the Lord Chancellor to hear such applications.

14E   Any application for a warrant which would take the period of detention beyond 14 days from the time of arrest (or if a person was being detained under TACT Schedule 7, from the time at which the examination under Schedule 7 began), must be made to a High Court Judge.

14F   If an application has been made to a High Court judge for a warrant which would take detention beyond 14 days, and the High Court judge instead issues a warrant for a period of time which would not take detention beyond 14 days, further applications for extension of detention must also be made to a High Court judge, regardless of the period of time to which they refer.

14G   TACT Schedule 8 Paragraph 31 requires a notice to be given to the detained person if a warrant is sought for further detention. This must be provided before the judicial hearing of the application for that warrant and must include:

a)   notification that the application for a warrant has been made

b)   the time at which the application was made

c)   the time at which the application is to be heard

d)   the grounds on which further detention is sought.

A notice must also be provided each time an application is made to extend an existing warrant

14H   An officer applying for an order under TACT Schedule 8 Paragraph 34 to withhold specified information on which he intends to rely when applying for a warrant of further detention, may make the application for the order orally or in writing. The most appropriate method of application will depend on the circumstances of the case and the need to ensure fairness to the detainee.

14I   Where facilities exist, hearings relating to extension of detention under Part III of Schedule 8 may take place using video conferencing facilities provided that the requirements set out in Schedule 8 are still met. However, if the judicial authority requires the detained person to be physically present at any hearing, this should be complied with as soon as practicable. Paragraphs 33(4) to 33(9) of TACT Schedule 8 govern the relevant conduct of hearings.

14J   Transfer to prison is intended to ensure that individuals who are detained for extended periods of time are held in a place designed for longer periods of detention than police *stations. Prison will provide detainees with a greater range of facilities more appropriate to longer detention periods.*

14K *The Code will only apply as is appropriate to the conditions of detention during the period of transit. There is obviously no requirement to provide such things as bed linen or reading materials for the journey between prison and police station.*

15 Charging

15.1 Charging of detained persons is covered by PACE and guidance issued under PACE by the Director of Public Prosecutions. General guidance on charging can be found in section 16 of PACE Code C.

16 Testing persons for the presence of specified Class A drugs

16.1 The provisions for drug testing under section 63B of PACE (as amended by section 5 of the Criminal Justice Act 2003 and section 7 of the Drugs Act 2005), do not apply to detention under TACT section 41 and Schedule 8. Guidance on these provisions can be found in section 17 of PACE Code C.

ANNEX A – INTIMATE AND STRIP SEARCHES

A   *Intimate search*

1.   An intimate search consists of the physical examination of a person's body orifices other than the mouth. The intrusive nature of such searches means the actual and potential risks associated with intimate searches must never be underestimated.

(a)   *Action*

2.   Body orifices other than the mouth may be searched only if authorised by an officer of inspector rank or above who has reasonable grounds for believing that the person may have concealed on themselves anything which they could and might use to cause physical injury to themselves or others at the station and the officer has reasonable grounds for believing that an intimate search is the only means of removing those items.

3.   Before the search begins, a police officer, designated detention officer or staff custody officer, must tell the detainee:-

   (a)   that the authority to carry out the search has been given;

   (b)   the grounds for giving the authorisation and for believing that the article cannot be removed without an intimate search.

4.   An intimate search may only be carried out by a registered medical practitioner or registered nurse, unless an officer of at least inspector rank considers this is not practicable, in which case a police officer may carry out the search. See *Notes A1 to A5*

5.   Any proposal for a search under *paragraph 2* to be carried out by someone other than a registered medical practitioner or registered nurse must only be considered as a last resort and when the authorising officer is satisfied the risks associated with allowing the item to remain with the detainee outweigh the risks associated with removing it. See *Notes A1 to A5*

6.   An intimate search at a police station of a juvenile or mentally disordered or otherwise mentally vulnerable person may take place only in the presence of an appropriate adult of the same sex, unless the detainee specifically requests a particular adult of the opposite sex who is readily available. In the case of a juvenile the search may take place in the absence of the appropriate adult only if the juvenile signifies in the presence of the appropriate adult they do not want the adult present during the search and the adult agrees. A record shall be made of the juvenile's decision and signed by the appropriate adult.

7. When an intimate search under *paragraph 2* is carried out by a police officer, the officer must be of the same sex as the detainee. A minimum of two people, other than the detainee, must be present during the search. Subject to *paragraph 6*, no person of the opposite sex who is not a medical practitioner or nurse shall be present, nor shall anyone whose presence is unnecessary. The search shall be conducted with proper regard to the sensitivity and vulnerability of the detainee.

(b)   Documentation

8. In the case of an intimate search under paragraph 2, the following shall be recorded as soon as practicable, in the detainee's custody record:

    • the authorisation to carry out the search;

    • the grounds for giving the authorisation;

    • the grounds for believing the article could not be removed without an intimate search

    • which parts of the detainee's body were searched

    • who carried out the search

    • who was present

    • the result.

9. If an intimate search is carried out by a police officer, the reason why it was impracticable for a registered medical practitioner or registered nurse to conduct it must be recorded.

B   Strip search

10. A strip search is a search involving the removal of more than outer clothing. In this Code, outer clothing includes shoes and socks.

(a)   Action

11. A strip search may take place only if it is considered necessary to remove an article which a detainee would not be allowed to keep, and the officer reasonably considers the detainee might have concealed such an article. Strip searches shall not be routinely carried out if there is no reason to consider that articles are concealed.

The conduct of strip searches

12.   When strip searches are conducted:

(a)   a police officer carrying out a strip search must be the same sex as the detainee;

(b)   the search shall take place in an area where the detainee cannot be seen by anyone who does not need to be present, nor by a member of the opposite sex except an appropriate adult who has been specifically requested by the detainee;

(c)   except in cases of urgency, where there is risk of serious harm to the detainee or to others, whenever a strip search involves exposure of intimate body parts, there must be at least two people present other than the detainee, and if the search is of a juvenile or mentally disordered or otherwise mentally vulnerable person, one of the people must be the appropriate adult. Except in urgent cases as above, a search of a juvenile may take place in the absence of the appropriate adult only if the juvenile signifies in the presence of the appropriate adult that they do not want the adult to be present during the search and the adult agrees. A record shall be made of the juvenile's decision and signed by the appropriate adult. The presence of more than two people, other than an appropriate adult, shall be permitted only in the most exceptional circumstances;

(d)   the search shall be conducted with proper regard to the sensitivity and vulnerability of the detainee in these circumstances and every reasonable effort shall be made to secure the detainee's co-operation and minimise embarrassment. Detainees who are searched shall not normally be required to remove all their clothes at the same time, e.g. a person should be allowed to remove clothing above the waist and redress before removing further clothing;

(e)   if necessary to assist the search, the detainee may be required to hold their arms in the air or to stand with their legs apart and bend forward so a visual examination may be made of the genital and anal areas provided no physical contact is made with any body orifice;

(f)   if articles are found, the detainee shall be asked to hand them over. If articles are found within any body orifice other than the mouth, and the detainee refuses to hand them over, their removal would constitute an intimate search, which must be carried out as in *Part A*;

(g)   a strip search shall be conducted as quickly as possible, and the detainee allowed to dress as soon as the procedure is complete.

(b) Documentation

13. A record shall be made on the custody record of a strip search including the reason it was considered necessary, those present and any result.

Notes for guidance

A1 *Before authorising any intimate search, the authorising officer must make every reasonable effort to persuade the detainee to hand the article over without a search. If the detainee agrees, a registered medical practitioner or registered nurse should whenever possible be asked to assess the risks involved and, if necessary, attend to assist the detainee.*

A2 *If the detainee does not agree to hand the article over without a search, the authorising officer must carefully review all the relevant factors before authorising an intimate search. In particular, the officer must consider whether the grounds for believing an article may be concealed are reasonable.*

A3 *If authority is given for a search under paragraph 2, a registered medical practitioner or registered nurse shall be consulted whenever possible. The presumption should be that the search will be conducted by the registered medical practitioner or registered nurse and the authorising officer must make every reasonable effort to persuade the detainee to allow the medical practitioner or nurse to conduct the search.*

A4 *A constable should only be authorised to carry out a search as a last resort and when all other approaches have failed. In these circumstances, the authorising officer must be satisfied the detainee might use the article for one or more of the purposes in paragraph 2 and the physical injury likely to be caused is sufficiently severe to justify authorising a constable to carry out the search.*

A5 *If an officer has any doubts whether to authorise an intimate search by a constable, the officer should seek advice from an officer of superintendent rank or above.*

H

ANNEX B – DELAY IN NOTIFYING ARREST OR ALLOWING ACCESS TO LEGAL ADVICE FOR PERSONS DETAINED UNDER THE TERRORISM ACT 2000.

A   *Delays under TACT Schedule 8*

1.   The rights as in *sections 5* or *6,* may be delayed if the person is detained under the Terrorism Act 2000, section 41, has not yet been charged with an offence and an officer of superintendent rank or above has reasonable grounds for believing the exercise of either right will have one of the following consequences:

   (a)   interference with or harm to evidence of a serious offence,

   (b)   interference with or physical injury to any person,

   (c)   the alerting of persons who are suspected of having committed a serious offence but who have not been arrested for it,

   (d)   the hindering of the recovery of property obtained as a result of a serious offence or in respect of which a forfeiture order could be made under section 23,

   (e)   interference with the gathering of information about the commission, preparation or instigation of acts of terrorism,

   (f)   the alerting of a person and thereby making it more difficult to prevent an act of terrorism, or

   (g)   the alerting of a person and thereby making it more difficult to secure a person's apprehension, prosecution or conviction in connection with the commission, preparation or instigation of an act of terrorism.

2.   These rights may also be delayed if the officer has reasonable grounds for believing that:

   (a)   the detained person has benefited from his criminal conduct (to be decided in accordance with Part 2 of the Proceeds of Crime Act 2002), and

   (b)   the recovery of the value of the property constituting the benefit will be hindered by—

      (i)   informing the named person of the detained person's detention (in the case of an authorisation under Paragraph 8(1)(a) of Schedule 8 to TACT, or

      (ii)   the exercise of the right under paragraph 7 (in the case of an authorisation under Paragraph 8(1)(b) of Schedule 8 to TACT.

3. Authority to delay a detainee's right to consult privately with a solicitor may be given only if the authorising officer has reasonable grounds to believe the solicitor the detainee wants to consult will, inadvertently or otherwise, pass on a message from the detainee or act in some other way which will have any of the consequences specified under *paragraph 8 of Schedule 8 to the Terrorism Act 2000*. In these circumstances the detainee must be allowed to choose another solicitor. See *Note B3*

4. If the detainee wishes to see a solicitor, access to that solicitor may not be delayed on the grounds they might advise the detainee not to answer questions or the solicitor was initially asked to attend the police station by someone else. In the latter case the detainee must be told the solicitor has come to the police station at another person's request, and must be asked to sign the custody record to signify whether they want to see the solicitor.

5. The fact the grounds for delaying notification of arrest may be satisfied does not automatically mean the grounds for delaying access to legal advice will also be satisfied.

6. These rights may be delayed only for as long as is necessary but not beyond 48 hours from the time of arrest (or if a person was being detained under TACT Schedule 7, from the time at which the examination under Schedule 7 began). If the above grounds cease to apply within this time the detainee must as soon as practicable be asked if they wish to exercise either right, the custody record noted accordingly, and action taken in accordance with the relevant section of this Code.

7. A person must be allowed to consult a solicitor for a reasonable time before any court hearing.

B   **Documentation**

8. The grounds for action under this Annex shall be recorded and the detainee informed of them as soon as practicable.

9. Any reply given by a detainee under *paragraph 6* must be recorded and the detainee asked to endorse the record in relation to whether they want to receive legal advice at this point.

C   **Cautions and special warnings**

10. When a suspect detained at a police station is interviewed during any period for which access to legal advice has been delayed under this Annex, the court or jury may not draw adverse inferences from their silence.

H

Notes for guidance

B1   *Even if Annex B applies in the case of a juvenile, or a person who is mentally disordered or otherwise mentally vulnerable, action to inform the appropriate adult and the person responsible for a juvenile's welfare if that is a different person, must nevertheless be taken as in paragraph 3.15 and 3.17.*

B2   *In the case of Commonwealth citizens and foreign nationals, see Note 7A.*

B3   *A decision to delay access to a specific solicitor is likely to be a rare occurrence and only when it can be shown the suspect is capable of misleading that particular solicitor and there is more than a substantial risk that the suspect will succeed in causing information to be conveyed which will lead to one or more of the specified consequences.*

ANNEX C – RESTRICTION ON DRAWING ADVERSE INFERENCES FROM SILENCE AND TERMS OF THE CAUTION WHEN THE RESTRICTION APPLIES

(a) *The restriction on drawing adverse inferences from silence*

1. The Criminal Justice and Public Order Act 1994, sections 34, 36 and 37 as amended by the Youth Justice and Criminal Evidence Act 1999, section 58 describe the conditions under which adverse inferences may be drawn from a person's failure or refusal to say anything about their involvement in the offence when interviewed, after being charged or informed they may be prosecuted. These provisions are subject to an overriding restriction on the ability of a court or jury to draw adverse inferences from a person's silence. This restriction applies:

    (a) to any detainee at a police station who, before being interviewed, see *section 11* or being charged or informed they may be prosecuted, see *section 15,* has:

        (i)   asked for legal advice, see *section 6, paragraph 6.1*;

        (ii) not been allowed an opportunity to consult a solicitor, including the duty solicitor, as in this Code; and

        (iii) not changed their mind about wanting legal advice, see *section 6, paragraph 6.7(c)*

        Note the condition in (ii) will

        –   apply when a detainee who has asked for legal advice is interviewed before speaking to a solicitor as in *section 6, paragraph 6.6(a)* or *(b)*.

        –   not apply if the detained person declines to ask for the duty solicitor, see *section 6, paragraphs 6.7(b)* and *(c)*;

    (b) to any person charged with, or informed they may be prosecuted for, an offence who:

        (i)   has had brought to their notice a written statement made by another person or the content of an interview with another person which relates to that offence, see PACE Code C *section 16, paragraph 16.6*;

        (ii) is interviewed about that offence, see PACE Code C *section 16, paragraph 16.8*; or

        (iii) makes a written statement about that offence, see *Annex D paragraphs 4* and *9*.

(b) *Terms of the caution when the restriction applies*

2.   When a requirement to caution arises at a time when the restriction on drawing adverse inferences from silence applies, the caution shall be:

'You do not have to say anything, but anything you do say may be given in evidence.'

3.   Whenever the restriction either begins to apply or ceases to apply after a caution has already been given, the person shall be re-cautioned in the appropriate terms. The changed position on drawing inferences and that the previous caution no longer applies shall also be explained to the detainee in ordinary language. See *Note C1*

Notes for guidance

C1   *The following is suggested as a framework to help explain changes in the position on drawing adverse inferences if the restriction on drawing adverse inferences from silence:*

(a)   *begins to apply:*

'The caution you were previously given no longer applies. This is because after that caution:

(i)   *you asked to speak to a solicitor but have not yet been allowed an opportunity to speak to a solicitor. See paragraph 1(a); or*

(ii)   *you have been charged with/informed you may be prosecuted. See paragraph 1(b).*

'This means that from now on, adverse inferences cannot be drawn at court and your defence will not be harmed just because you choose to say nothing. Please listen carefully to the caution I am about to give you because it will apply from now on. You will see that it does not say anything about your defence being harmed.'

(b)   *ceases to apply before or at the time the person is charged or informed they may be prosecuted, see paragraph 1(a);*

'The caution you were previously given no longer applies. This is because after that caution you have been allowed an opportunity to speak to a solicitor. Please listen carefully to the caution I am about to give you because it will apply from now on. It explains how your defence at court may be affected if you choose to say nothing.'

ANNEX D – WRITTEN STATEMENTS UNDER CAUTION

(a) *Written by a person under caution*

1. A person shall always be invited to write down what they want to say.

2. A person who has not been charged with, or informed they may be prosecuted for, any offence to which the statement they want to write relates, shall:

    (a) unless the statement is made at a time when the restriction on drawing adverse inferences from silence applies, see Annex C, be asked to write out and sign the following before writing what they want to say:

        'I make this statement of my own free will. I understand that I do not have to say anything but that it may harm my defence if I do not mention when questioned something which I later rely on in court. This statement may be given in evidence.';

    (b) If the statement is made at a time when the restriction on drawing adverse inferences from silence applies, be asked to write out and sign the following before writing what they want to say;

        'I make this statement of my own free will. I understand that I do not have to say anything. This statement may be given in evidence.'

3. When a person, on the occasion of being charged with or informed they may be prosecuted for any offence, asks to make a statement which relates to any such offence and wants to write it they shall:

    (a) unless the restriction on drawing adverse inferences from silence, see *Annex C*, applied when they were so charged or informed they may be prosecuted, be asked to write out and sign the following before writing what they want to say:

        'I make this statement of my own free will. I understand that I do not have to say anything but that it may harm my defence If I do not mention when questioned something which I later rely on in court. This statement may be given in evidence.';

    (b) if the restriction on drawing adverse inferences from silence applied when they were so charged or informed they may be prosecuted, be asked to write out and sign the following before writing what they want to say:

        'I make this statement of my own free will. I understand that I do not have to say anything. This statement may be given in evidence.'

H

4. When a person, who has already been charged with or informed they may be prosecuted for any offence, asks to make a statement which relates to any such offence and wants to write it they shall be asked to write out and sign the following before writing what they want to say:

> *'I make this statement of my own free will. I understand that I do not have to say anything. This statement may be given in evidence.';*

5. Any person writing their own statement shall be allowed to do so without any prompting except a police officer or other police staff may indicate to them which matters are material or question any ambiguity in the statement.

(b) Written by a police officer or other police staff

6. If a person says they would like someone to write the statement for them, a police officer, or other police staff shall write the statement.

7. If the person has not been charged with, or informed they may be prosecuted for, any offence to which the statement they want to make relates they shall, before starting, be asked to sign, or make their mark, to the following:

(a) unless the statement is made at a time when the restriction on drawing adverse inferences from silence applies, see *Annex C*:

> *'I, ..., wish to make a statement. I want someone to write down what I say. I understand that I do not have to say anything but that it may harm my defence if I do not mention when questioned something which I later rely on in court. This statement may be given in evidence.';*

(b) if the statement is made at a time when the restriction on drawing adverse inferences from silence applies:

> *'I, ..., wish to make a statement. I want someone to write down what I say. I understand that I do not have to say anything. This statement may be given in evidence.'*

8. If, on the occasion of being charged with or informed they may be prosecuted for any offence, the person asks to make a statement which relates to any such offence they shall before starting be asked to sign, or make their mark to, the following:

(a) unless the restriction on drawing adverse inferences from silence applied, see *Annex C,* when they were so charged or informed they may be prosecuted:

'I, ..., wish to make a statement. I want someone to write down what I say. I understand that I do not have to say anything but that it may harm my defence if I do not mention when questioned something which I later rely on in court. This statement may be given in evidence.';

(b)   if the restriction on drawing adverse inferences from silence applied when they were so charged or informed they may be prosecuted:

'I, ..., wish to make a statement. I want someone to write down what I say. I understand that I do not have to say anything. This statement may be given in evidence.'

9.   If, having already been charged with or informed they may be prosecuted for any offence, a person asks to make a statement which relates to any such offence they shall before starting, be asked to sign, or make their mark to:

'I, ..., wish to make a statement. I want someone to write down what I say. I understand that I do not have to say anything. This statement may be given in evidence.'

10.   The person writing the statement must take down the exact words spoken by the person making it and must not edit or paraphrase it. Any questions that are necessary, e.g. to make it more intelligible, and the answers given must be recorded at the same time on the statement form.

11.   When the writing of a statement is finished the person making it shall be asked to read it and to make any corrections, alterations or additions they want. When they have finished reading they shall be asked to write and sign or make their mark on the following certificate at the end of the statement:

'I have read the above statement, and I have been able to correct, alter or add anything I wish. This statement is true. I have made it of my own free will.'

12.   If the person making the statement cannot read, or refuses to read it, or to write the above mentioned certificate at the end of it or to sign it, the person taking the statement shall read it to them and ask them if they would like to correct, alter or add anything and to put their signature or make their mark at the end. The person taking the statement shall certify on the statement itself what has occurred.

ANNEX E – SUMMARY OF PROVISIONS RELATING TO MENTALLY DISORDERED AND OTHERWISE MENTALLY VULNERABLE PEOPLE

1. If an officer has any suspicion, or is told in good faith, that a person of any age may be mentally disordered or otherwise mentally vulnerable, or mentally incapable of understanding the significance of questions or their replies that person shall be treated as mentally disordered or otherwise mentally vulnerable for the purposes of this Code. See *paragraph 1.10*

2. In the case of a person who is mentally disordered or otherwise mentally vulnerable, 'the appropriate adult' means:

    (a) a relative, guardian or other person responsible for their care or custody;

    (b) someone experienced in dealing with mentally disordered or mentally vulnerable people but who is not a police officer or employed by the police;

    (c) failing these, some other responsible adult aged 18 or over who is not a police officer or employed by the police.

    See *paragraph 1.13(b) and Note 1D*

3. If the detention of a person who is mentally vulnerable or appears to be suffering from a mental disorder is authorised by the review officer (see *paragraphs 14.1* and *14.2* and *Notes for Guidance 14A* and *14B)* , the custody officer must as soon as practicable inform the appropriate adult of the grounds for detention and the person's whereabouts, and ask the adult to come to the police station to see them. If the appropriate adult:

    • is already at the station when information is given as in *paragraphs 3.1* to *3.5* the information must be given in their presence

    • is not at the station when the provisions of *paragraph 3.1* to *3.5* are complied with these provisions must be complied with again in their presence once they arrive.

    See *paragraphs 3.15* to *3.16*

4. If the appropriate adult, having been informed of the right to legal advice, considers legal advice should be taken, the provisions of *section 6* apply as if the mentally disordered or otherwise mentally vulnerable person had requested access to legal advice. See *paragraph 3.20* and *Note E1*.

5. The custody officer must make sure a person receives appropriate clinical attention as soon as reasonably practicable if the person appears to be suffering from a mental disorder or in urgent cases immediately call the nearest health care professional or an ambulance. It is not intended these provisions delay the transfer of a detainee to a

place of safety under the Mental Health Act 1983, section 136 if that is applicable. If an assessment under that Act is to take place at a police station, the custody officer must consider whether an appropriate health care professional should be called to conduct an initial clinical check on the detainee. See *paragraph 9.6* and *9.8*

6.   If a mentally disordered or otherwise mentally vulnerable person is cautioned in the absence of the appropriate adult, the caution must be repeated in the appropriate adult's presence. See *paragraph 10.11*

7.   A mentally disordered or otherwise mentally vulnerable person must not be interviewed or asked to provide or sign a written statement in the absence of the appropriate adult unless the provisions of *paragraphs 11.2* or *11.11 to 11.13* apply. Questioning in these circumstances may not continue in the absence of the appropriate adult once sufficient information to avert the risk has been obtained. A record shall be made of the grounds for any decision to begin an interview in these circumstances. See *paragraphs 11.2, 11.9* and *11.11 to 11.13*

8.   If the appropriate adult is present at an interview, they shall be informed they are not expected to act simply as an observer and the purposes of their presence are to:

•   advise the interviewee

•   observe whether or not the interview is being conducted properly and fairly

•   facilitate communication with the interviewee

See *paragraph 11.10*

9.   If the custody officer charges a mentally disordered or otherwise mentally vulnerable person with an offence or takes such other action as is appropriate when there is sufficient evidence for a prosecution this must be done in the presence of the appropriate adult. The written notice embodying any charge must be given to the appropriate adult. See *paragraphs PACE Code C Section 16.*

10.   An intimate or strip search of a mentally disordered or otherwise mentally vulnerable person may take place only in the presence of the appropriate adult of the same sex, unless the detainee specifically requests the presence of a particular adult of the opposite sex. A strip search may take place in the absence of an appropriate adult only in cases of urgency when there is a risk of serious harm to the detainee or others. See *Annex A, paragraphs 6* and *12(c)*

11.   Particular care must be taken when deciding whether to use any form of approved restraints on a mentally disordered or otherwise mentally vulnerable person in a locked cell. See *paragraph 8.2*

Notes for guidance

E1   *The purpose of the provision at paragraph 3.20 is to protect the rights of a mentally disordered or otherwise mentally vulnerable detained person who does not understand the significance of what is said to them. If the detained person wants to exercise the right to legal advice, the appropriate action should be taken and not delayed until the appropriate adult arrives. A mentally disordered or otherwise mentally vulnerable detained person should always be given an opportunity, when an appropriate adult is called to the police station, to consult privately with a solicitor in the absence of the appropriate adult if they want.*

E2   *Although people who are mentally disordered or otherwise mentally vulnerable are often capable of providing reliable evidence, they may, without knowing or wanting to do so, be particularly prone in certain circumstances to provide information that may be unreliable, misleading or self-incriminating. Special care should always be taken when questioning such a person, and the appropriate adult should be involved if there is any doubt about a person's mental state or capacity. Because of the risk of unreliable evidence, it is important to obtain corroboration of any facts admitted whenever possible.*

E3   *Because of the risks referred to in Note E2, which the presence of the appropriate adult is intended to minimise, officers of superintendent rank or above should exercise their discretion to authorise the commencement of an interview in the appropriate adult's absence only in exceptional cases, if it is necessary to avert an immediate risk of serious harm. See paragraphs 11.2, 11.11 to 11.13*

ANNEX F – COUNTRIES WITH WHICH BILATERAL CONSULAR CONVENTIONS OR AGREEMENTS REQUIRING NOTIFICATION OF THE ARREST AND DETENTION OF THEIR NATIONALS ARE IN FORCE.

H

Armenia

Austria

Azerbaijan

Belarus

Belgium

Bosnia-Herzegovina

Bulgaria

China*

Croatia

Ouba

Czech Republic

Denmark

Egypt

France

Georgia

German Federal Republic

Greece

Hungary

Italy

Japan

Kazakhstan

Macedonia

Mexico

Moldova

Mongolia

Norway

Poland

Romania

Russia

Slovak Republic

Slovenia

Spain

Sweden

Tajikistan

Turkmenistan

Ukraine

USA

Uzbekistan

Yugoslavia

* Police are required to inform Chinese officials of arrest/detention in the Manchester consular district only. This comprises Derbyshire, Durham, Greater Manchester, Lancashire, Merseyside, North South and West Yorkshire, and Tyne and Wear.

ANNEX G – FITNESS TO BE INTERVIEWED

1.   This Annex contains general guidance to help police officers and health care professionals assess whether a detainee might be at risk in an interview.

2.   A detainee may be at risk in a interview if it is considered that:

   (a)   conducting the interview could significantly harm the detainee's physical or mental state;

   (b)   anything the detainee says in the interview about their involvement or suspected involvement in the offence about which they are being interviewed **might** be considered unreliable in subsequent court proceedings because of their physical or mental state.

3.   In assessing whether the detainee should be interviewed, the following must be considered:

   (a)   how the detainee's physical or mental state might affect their ability to understand the nature and purpose of the interview, to comprehend what is being asked and to appreciate the significance of any answers given and make rational decisions about whether they want to say anything;

   (b)   the extent to which the detainee's replies may be affected by their physical or mental condition rather than representing a rational and accurate explanation of their involvement in the offence;

   (c)   how the nature of the interview, which could include particularly probing questions, might affect the detainee.

4.   It is essential health care professionals who are consulted consider the functional ability of the detainee rather than simply relying on a medical diagnosis, e.g. it is possible for a person with severe mental illness to be fit for interview.

5.   Health care professionals should advise on the need for an appropriate adult to be present, whether reassessment of the person's fitness for interview may be necessary if the interview lasts beyond a specified time, and whether a further specialist opinion may be required.

6.   When health care professionals identify risks they should be asked to quantify the risks. They should inform the custody officer:

   •   whether the person's condition:

      –   is likely to improve

      –   will require or be amenable to treatment; and

      •   indicate how long it may take for such improvement to take effect

7.   The role of the health care professional is to consider the risks and advise the custody officer of the outcome of that consideration. The health care professional's determination and any advice or recommendations should be made in writing and form part of the custody record.

8.   Once the health care professional has provided that information, it is a matter for the custody officer to decide whether or not to allow the interview to go ahead and if the interview is to proceed, to determine what safeguards are needed. Nothing prevents safeguards being provided in addition to those required under the Code. An example might be to have an appropriate health care professional present during the interview, in addition to an appropriate adult, in order constantly to monitor the person's condition and how it is being affected by the interview.

H

ANNEX H – DETAINED PERSON: OBSERVATION LIST

H

1. If any detainee fails to meet any of the following criteria, an appropriate health care professional or an ambulance must be called.

2. When assessing the level of rousability, consider:

   Rousability – can they be woken?

   - go into the cell
   - call their name
   - shake gently

   Response to questions – can they give appropriate answers to questions such as:

   - What's your name?
   - Where do you live?
   - Where do you think you are?

   Response to commands – can they respond appropriately to commands such as:

   - Open your eyes!
   - Lift one arm, now the other arm!

3. Remember to take into account the possibility or presence of other illnesses, injury, or mental condition, a person who is drowsy and smells of alcohol may also have the following:

   - Diabetes
   - Epilepsy
   - Head injury
   - Drug intoxication or overdose
   - Stroke